SCORPIO 2002

By the same author

Teri King's Complete Guide to Your Stars
Teri King's Astrological Horoscopes for 2002:

Aries 21 March to 19 April
Taurus 20 April to 20 May
Gemini 21 May to 21 June
Cancer 22 June to 22 July
Leo 23 July to 22 August
Virgo 23 August to 22 September
Libra 23 September to 23 October
Sagittarius 22 November to 21 December
Capricorn 22 December to 19 January
Aquarius 20 January to 18 February
Pisces 19 February to 20 March

Teri King's Astrological Horoscopes for 2002

♏

Scorpio

Teri King's complete horoscope for all those whose birthdays fall between 24 October and 21 November

Teri King

Thorsons

Thorsons
An Imprint of HarperCollins*Publishers*
77–85 Fulham Palace Road
Hammersmith, London W6 8JB

The Thorsons website address is: www.thorsons.com

Published by Thorsons 2001

1 3 5 7 9 10 8 6 4 2

©Teri King 2001

Teri King asserts the moral right to be
identified as the author of this work

A catalogue record for this book
is available from the British Library

ISBN 0 00 712147 4

Printed and bound in Great Britain by
Omnia Books Limited, Glasgow

All rights reserved. No part of this publication may be
reproduced, stored in a retrieval system, or transmitted,
in any form or by any means, electronic, mechanical,
photocopying, recording or otherwise, without the prior
permission of the publishers.

Contents

Introduction **vii**

How Does Astrology Work? **1**

The Sun in Scorpio **4**

The Year Ahead: Overview **6**

Career Year **9**

Money Year **13**

Love and Sex Year **15**

Health and Diet Year **19**

Numerology Year **23**

Your Sun Sign Partner **44**

Monthly and Daily Guides **56**

♏

Scorpio
24 October to 21 November

Ruling Planet: **Pluto, Mars**
Element: **Water**
Quality: **Feminine**
Planetary Principle: **Power**
Primal Desire: **Control**
Colour: **Black, Purple**
Jewels: **Amethyst, Topaz**
Day: **Tuesday**
Magical Number: **Four**

Famous Scorpios
Theodore Roosevelt, Anita Roddick, Bill Wyman, Bob Hoskins, Jaclyn Smith, John Cleese, Simon Le Bon, Joan Plowright, Julia Roberts, Michael Winner, Princess Marina, Viscount Linley, Tatum O'Neal.

Introduction

Astrology has many uses, not least of these its ability to help us to understand both ourselves and other people. Unfortunately there are many misconceptions and confusions associated with it, such as that old chestnut – how can a zodiac forecast be accurate for all the millions of people born under one particular sign?

The answer to this is that all horoscopes published in newspapers, books and magazines are, of necessity, of a general nature. Unless an astrologer can work from the date, time and place of your birth, the reading given will only be true for the typical member of your sign.

For instance, let's take a person born on 9 August. This person is principally a subject of Leo, simply because the Sun occupied that section of the heavens known as Leo during 23 July to 22 August. However, when delving into astrology at its most serious, there are other influences which need to be taken into consideration – for example, the Moon. This planet enters a fresh sign every 48 hours. On the birth date in question it may have been in, say, Virgo. And if this were the case it would make our particular subject Leo (Sun representing willpower) and Virgo (Moon representing instincts) or, if you will, a Leo/Virgo. Then again the rising sign of 'ascendant' must also be taken into consideration. This also changes constantly as the Earth revolves: approximately every two hours a new section of the heavens comes into view – a new sign passes over the horizon. The rising sign is of the utmost importance, determining the image projected by the subject to the outside world – in effect, the personality.

The time of birth is essential when compiling a birth chart. Let us suppose that in this particular instance Leo was rising at the time of birth. Now, because two of the three main influences are Leo, our sample case would be fairly typical of his or her sign, possessing all the faults and attributes associated with it. However, if the Moon and ascendant had been in Virgo then, whilst our subject would certainly display some of the Leo attributes or faults, it is more than likely that for the most part he or she would feel and behave more like a Virgoan.

As if life weren't complicated enough, this procedure must be carried through to take into account all the remaining planets. The position and signs of Mercury, Venus, Mars, Jupiter, Saturn, Uranus, Neptune and Pluto must all be discovered, plus the aspect formed from one planet to another. The calculation and interpretation of these movements by an astrologer will then produce an individual birth chart.

Because the heavens are constantly changing, people with identical charts are a very rare occurrence. Although it is not inconceivable that it could happen, this would mean that the two subjects were born not only on the same date and at the same time, but also in the same place. Should such an incident occur, then the deciding factors as to how these individuals would differ in their approach to life, love, career, financial prospects and so on, would be due to environmental and parental influence.

Returning to our hypothetical Leo: our example with the rising Sun in Leo and Moon in Virgo may find it useful not only to read up on his or her Sun sign (Leo) but also to read the section dealing with Virgo (the Moon). Nevertheless, this does not invalidate Sun sign astrology. This is because of the great power the Sun possesses, and on any chart this planet plays an important role.

Belief in astrology does not necessarily mean believing in totally determined lives – that our actions are predestined and we have no control over our fate. What it does clearly show is that our lives run in cycles, for both good and bad and, with the aid of astrology, we can make the most of, or minimize, certain patterns and tendencies. How this is done is entirely up to the individual. For example, if you are in possession of the knowledge that you are about to experience a lucky few days or weeks, then you can make the most of them by pushing ahead with plans. You can also be better prepared for illness, misfortune, romantic upset and every adversity.

Astrology should be used as it was originally intended – as a guide, especially to character. In this direction it is invaluable and it can help us in all aspects of friendship, work and romance. It makes it easier for us to see ourselves as we really are and, what's more, as others see us. We can recognize both our own weaknesses and strengths and those of others. It can give us both outer confidence and inner peace.

In the following pages you will find personality profiles, an in-depth look at the year ahead from all possible angles including numerology, monthly and daily guides, your Sun sign partner, plus, and it is a big plus, information for those poor and confused creatures so often ignored who are born on 'the cusp' – at the beginning or the end of each sign.

Used wisely, astrology can help you through life. It is not intended to encourage complacency, since, in the final analysis, what you do with your life is up to you. This book will aid you in adopting the correct attitude to the year ahead and thus maximize your chances of success. Positive thinking is encouraged because this helps us to attract positive situations. Allow astrology to walk hand in hand with you and you will be increasing your chances of success and happiness.

How Does Astrology Work?

You often hear people say that there is no scientific explanation for astrology. However, astrological calculations may be explained in a very precise way, and they can be done by anyone with a little practice and a knowledge of the movement of stars and planets. It is the interpretations and conclusions drawn from these observations that are not necessarily consistent or verifiable, and, to be sure, predicted events do not always happen. Yet astrology has lasted in our culture for over 3,000 years, so there must be something in it!

So how can we explain astrology? Well, each individual birth sign has its own set of deep-seated characteristics, and an understanding of these can give you fresh insights into why you behave as you do. Reading an astrological interpretation, even if it is just to find out how, say, a new relationship might develop, means that you should think about yourself in a very deep way. But it is important to remember that the stars don't determine your fate. It is up to you to use them to the best advantage in any situation.

Although astrology, like many other 'alternative' practices such as homeopathy, dowsing and telepathy, cannot completely be explained, there have been convincing experiments that have shown that it works far more often than chance would allow. The best-known studies are those of the French statistician, Michel Gauquelin, whose results were checked by a professor at the University of London who declared, grudgingly, that 'there was something in it'.

An important aspect of astrology is to look at how the Sun and the Moon affect the natural world around us from day to day. For instance, the rise and fall of the tides is purely a result of the movement and position of the Moon relative to the Earth. If this massive magnetic pull can move the oceans of the Earth, what does it do to us? After all, we are, on average, over 60 per cent water!

When it comes to the ways in which the Sun may change the world, a whole book could be written on the subject. The influences we know about include day length, heat, light, solar storms, as well as magnetic, ultra-violet and many other forms of radiation. And all this from over 90 million miles away! For example, observation of birds has shown that before migration – governed by changes in the length of days – birds put on extra layers of fat, and that they experience a nocturnal restlessness shortly before setting off on their travels. I'm not suggesting that we put on weight and experience sleepless nights because of the time of year, but many people will tell you that different seasons affect them in different ways.

Another example from the natural world is a curious species of giant worm which lives in underground caverns in the South Pacific. Twice a year, as the Sun is rising and the tide is at its highest, these worms come to the surface of the ocean. The inhabitants of the islands consider them a great delicacy! There are so many instances of creatures on this planet responding to the influences of the Moon and the Sun that it is only common sense to wonder whether the position of other planets also has an affect, even if it is more subtle and less easy to identify.

Finally, we come to the question of how astrology might work in predicting future events. As we have seen, the planetary bodies are likely to affect us in all sorts of ways, both physically and mentally. Most often, subtle changes in the positions of the planets will cause slight changes in our emotional states and, of course, this will affect how we behave. By drawing up a chart based on precise birth times, and by using their intuition, some astrologers can make precise predictions about how planetary influences in the years ahead are likely to shape the life of an individual. Many people are very surprised at how well an astrologer seems to 'understand' them after reading a commentary on their birth chart!

Stranger still are the astrologers who appear to be able to predict future events many years before they happen. The most famous example of all is the 16th-century French astrologer, Nostradamus, who is well-known for having predicted the possibility of world destruction at the end of the last millennium. Don't worry, I think I can cheerfully put everyone's mind at rest by assuring you that the world will go on for a good many years yet. Although Nostradamus certainly made some very accurate predictions in his lifetime, his prophecies for our future are very obscure and are hotly disputed by all the experts. Mind you, it is quite clear that there are likely to be massive changes ahead. It is a possibility, for instance, that information may come to light about past civilizations, now at the bottom of the Mediterranean Sea: this will give us a good idea about how people once lived in the past, and pointers as to how we should live in the future. Try not to fear, dear reader. Astrology is a tool for us to use and if we use it wisely, no doubt we will survive with greater wisdom and a greater respect for our world and each other.

The Sun in Scorpio

You are compassionate, psychic, intuitive and kind, and because of this you would never say no to a friend in need. Your vision is total truth, and with one penetrating glance you can see all. At a party, you can feel the pain of a laughing stranger and can understand the fears behind the smirk of his best friend.

You tend to be secretive, somewhat shy, and consider your privacy extremely sacred. Because you reveal so little of yourself in a social situation, you sometimes gain a reputation for being inscrutable. The fact is that you are cautious in all of your movements because you're so emotionally vulnerable. You feel so intensely that you erect safeguards to make sure your feelings don't undermine you.

Often there's a sternness in your character and a do-it-yourself attitude that sometimes drives those you love crazy. It's rare that you ask for help, and when it is offered, it is equally hard for you to accept it. Unlike other signs, you tend to be a loner, and of all the signs, you are probably the most self-sufficient, a quality in which you take great pride.

On a daily basis, you battle with the darker side where the mood swings seem to swallow you. However, with determination you usually overcome them to do what you have to do and do it to the best of your ability. Deep inside there is a hunger that has made you search for activities with greater meaning. You are highly intelligent, have a keen memory and a probing mind that restlessly looks for a broader understanding of the universe, and certainly of yourself. For this reason, as well as your extraordinary insight, you can be formidable, a psychotherapist as well as a psychic healer.

The problems that would make another person fall apart and throw up their hands, you face with calm, poise, dignity and a sense of self-possession. Any doubts you keep on the inside, while on the outside you are wilful, tenacious and exert a formidable influence in all of your undertakings. Your unusual qualities of endurance and perseverance and your strength of mind can take you through any crises and help you to grow with the unfolding of new and emotional situations.

However, should you find yourself in a romantic situation where you're beginning to lose more than you're getting, you will reach a point of frustration where your feelings cut off while your mind drifts to the possibility of a new lover. You never feel that you are compromising your fidelity if your frustrations tell you that you can only find what you need elsewhere. So ease yourself out of a decaying situation. Alternatively, by easing yourself out, you may force a confrontation that will make the relationship stronger in the long run. It is highly likely that hope was always part of your motivation.

The Year Ahead: Overview

This year, Pluto will be sizzling along in the fiery sign of Sagittarius, and this will stimulate your faith in human nature and could add some impulsiveness, enthusiasm and self-expenditure. Your sense of perspective will be good, and you will have the ability for exploration, versatility and happiness.

Pluto's placing in the financial area of your chart shows that there could be gains, and indeed losses, through sensational, unusual and adventurous channels. Many of you may have several sources of income, and those of you involved in mining, the armed forces or other uniformed occupations are certainly in for a good time. Regardless of what you do for a living, your ability will win high returns, but you must not squander them. Do make sure that financial considerations don't dominate your attitude to cash, or you could become obsessively unscrupulous.

For the entire year, Neptune will be drifting along in the sign of Aquarius; therefore, you'll be more responsive to social, political and philosophical stimuli. The placing of this planet seems to suggest that you will be challenging established security and could, on occasions, be naïvely self-absorbed. Travel is likely to be more frequent, and your ties

The Year Ahead: Overview

with parents could become a good deal closer. Domestically, you could be over-idealistic, and at times this will be exhausting to those you care about. Many of you will be improving your surroundings a good deal throughout this year.

Uranus, too, is making its way through Aquarius, awakening understanding and progressive thinking, though at the same time destroying any sentimentality that you may have. On occasions, your willpower could be somewhat erratic and wayward, and you will need to control a tendency to self-will and perversity.

The placing of Uranus could make your career a little bit chequered from time to time. What's more, parental influence may be more stimulating than usual, so listen to your family from time to time. On a domestic level, many sudden changes and strange experiences may occur, but you will turn this around positively; in fact, you will find it quite challenging and will be ready to take on board everything that is thrown at you.

All year Saturn will be in Gemini and that's the area of your chart devoted to big business, people you are financially dependent upon, and insurance matters. There could be some disappointments where these sides to life are concerned unless you double check everything. In this way you may be able to make life a little easier for yourself. However, being a Scorpio, with an eagle eye, you're probably going to do this without any encouragement from me anyway.

Lucky Jupiter will be drifting along in the water sign of Cancer up until 1 August. That's the area of your chart devoted to long-distance travelling, foreign affairs and legal matters, all of which will have a happy glow about them, so don't hesitate to push ahead in this side to life.

From 2 August to the end of the year, Jupiter will be in Leo and that, of course, is the zenith point of your chart, so where work and professional matters are concerned you're going to be falling on your feet more than once. However, you must be quick to snap up opportunities because they don't come around too often now, do they? So grab them with both hands and you'll be doing yourself the power of good during the remainder of this year.

Career Year

As a Scorpio, you're at your happiest when you are convinced that your work is of the utmost importance. Trivialities leave you cold: you prefer to deal with reality. Your eagle eye and talent for probing often lead you into research, and analysing or solving mysteries. It's essential that your clever and devious mind is channelled constructively: otherwise, you could very well be an excellent criminal. Rather, you should express these talents as a surgeon, detective, psychoanalyst, scientist or a lawyer. You need to tax your abilities to the fullest extent in whatever path you choose. Your jealousy can be the ruin of you; however, it could also act as a spur because you envy those in high positions, the privileged and those who are born to wealth. This causes you to strive for self-improvement, and your determination makes you a formidable opponent. Success means a great deal to you, but what you firstly consider to be success can be many different things.

If you are a more business-oriented kind of Scorpio, success means having immense power. You are driven, shrewd, organized and hard working, and highly focussed in all professional undertakings; unlike other signs, however, you don't have to shout from the top of the mountain to prove your position. Instead, you are quiet and calculating and you're content to pull all the strings from a place of luxurious privacy. There are many former presidents and prime ministers born under your sign, and this is not at all surprising, since the Scorpio mind is at once shrewd, wilful, tenacious, controlling, success-oriented and highly intelligent.

You could be anything from a hired killer to a surgeon, from an international spy to an insurance salesman, from a mortician to a psychoanalyst. After you've run through all of those, you could very well end up as a preacher. Even if you are sedentary, you think big thoughts.

But what about the year ahead?

Well, from 1 January to 19 January it's those of you who are involved in team effort, research, and any kind of association who will be doing well. If this applies to you, push ahead.

From 20 January to 18 February, the Sun will be drifting along in the sign of Aquarius, that's the area of your chart devoted to property and occupations connected with the home, whether it be a plumber, plasterer, furnishings, etc. If this applies to you, you'll be doing extremely well.

From 19 February to 20 March the Sun is in Pisces, so a good time for those of you who are artistic or in the entertainment business. However, during this time, you must not be tempted to gamble in any way, shape or form, otherwise you could become truly unstuck.

From 21 March to 19 April the Sun will, of course, be in Aries so, regardless of your work, you're going to be slaving away. Your workload will be heavy, and as an ambitious Scorpio you should be able to cope with literally anything – and you will.

From 20 April to 20 May, the Sun will be in earthy Taurus. That is, of course, your opposite number, and during this time partnerships of all descriptions will be going well. If you're in a professional relationship things will be going from good to better and you'll be feeling extremely optimistic.

From 21 May to 21 June, the Sun will be drifting along in the airy sign of Gemini. That is the area of your chart which rules big business, insurance matters and your relationships with your workmates, all of which will be flourishing.

From 22 June to 22 July the Sun is in Cancer, so all jobs related to matters connected with abroad, higher education and insurance will be flourishing.

From 23 July to 22 August, the Sun is situated in Leo and that is the zenith point of your chart, so your prestige and fortunes are likely to be on the up and up and you must take advantage of this, because it's not going to be lasting for too long.

From 23 August to 22 September, the Sun will be in Virgo. Good for those of you who work as part of a team such as farming, any jobs connected with bricks, mortar and the basics in life.

From 23 September to 23 October, the Sun is in the airy sign of Libra and that's a rather secretive part of your chart. It's good for those of you who work behind the scenes and those whose job relies upon intuition and instinct.

From 24 October to 21 November, the Sun is in the water sign of Scorpio. That, of course, is your sign, so regardless of your job, you're fiercely ambitious, fighting your way up the ladder of success and doing exceptionally well, and you're alert to any opportunities at this time.

From 22 November to 21 December, the Sun is in Sagittarius, the area of your chart devoted to money, so if you're in accountancy or any kind of monied profession others will be admiring your ambition and your thoroughness.

From 22 December to the end of the year, the Sun is in Capricorn, the area of your chart devoted to short journeys, buying and selling, so if you are a salesman who needs to impress customers, you'll be doing just that with a certain amount of aplomb.

All in all, this seems to be an extremely good year for professional matters.

Money Year

To you, money is certainly power. You feel it, you know it, but you find it hard to admit it honestly. Your sense of survival is paramount and you know how to make money last. You can live on next to nothing, but you don't enjoy doing so. Poverty is hardly one of your favourite pastimes, yet your inordinate pride and self-sufficiency can force you to forego a lot of little conveniences just to save your dignity.

There's a stern side to your character and that makes you choose to suffer in silence rather than humble yourself by asking for financial help. Of all the signs, you are the most able to sacrifice pleasant indulgences for future financial realization. Deep down, you see the process of gaining wealth as gaining supremacy in a power struggle; for you, though, the struggle is not against the establishment, but also against the unconscious part of you.

You heartily enjoy being associated with cash: not for its intrinsic value, but because it symbolizes a certain level of achievement. For you, money has no importance in itself. Its pursuit is merely a personal challenge, and possessing it is only a means to an end. What you gain from cash, beyond little luxuries and creature comforts, is a sense of satisfaction in having attained it. For you, gaining wealth is a game to test your personal power. It's a challenge, like chess, but with higher social stakes. You know that you'll always win. The key is staying cool and refusing to let it control you.

However, what about the year 2002 on the cash front?

Well, as you may know, this area of your life is ruled by lucky Jupiter, and that's why you so often fall on your feet.

Jupiter will be in the sign of Cancer up until 1 August, and that's the area of your chart devoted to further education, long distance travel, foreigners and ambition. Because Jupiter is a lucky planet, it's not surprising that you often find yourself in the right place, at the right time, and this year is no exception.

From 2 August to the end of the year, Jupiter will be in Leo which is the zenith point of your chart, the area which rules your profession, so quite clearly there is expansion going on where money matters are concerned and you should end this year very much on top providing, of course, you look out for the pitfalls which you can certainly find in this little book. The only danger really is through over-optimism and perhaps carelessness, but these are easily side-stepped as I have already suggested.

Be certain to grab all chances that come your way because they don't often come around twice, as you already know. Fortunately, as you are so ambitious, this is unlikely to happen and you should have a successful year.

Love and Sex Year

If you are a female Scorpio, you may be both more mysterious and more vulnerable than your male counterpart. While he can sublimate his emotions through work, sexual manipulations, and athletic prowess, you're generally not satisfied with anything less than an intense, meaningful kind of love.

Scorpio women are loyal and giving, and you can appear to be placid, even when your emotions are ripping your mind to pieces. At the same time, you're reluctant to lose control until you have shrewdly assessed the odds of every romantic situation. Unfortunately, sometimes your desires get the better of you, and you may find yourself emotionally tied to a horrible affair with no clear recollection of how you got there in the first place.

Your sex appeal is quiet, but exciting, and it emanates from your eyes. Your direct gaze and smile have a sensuality that can move a man to lust in less than a minute. Yet unlike your Scorpio brother, promiscuity is not your emotional forte. You seek security, tenderness and trust, and you are willing to give all of yourself in return for what you desire.

The Scorpio man is a warrior, especially in love; however, unlike his Martian sibling, Aries, he usually battles against his partner rather than for her. If you're a male Scorpio, you probably operate all your romantic endeavours from a mental control panel whose emotional switch is off. You're so inscrutable and emotionally maddening that a bad involvement with you is enough to send some sweet thing to a mental institution. Although you have a lot of loyalty, you are really not a prize in affairs of the heart. You seldom compliment, rarely communicate, and keep your feelings carefully closeted until the object of your affections is ready to sign her life away. And you want it written in blood.

Although you expect a kind of active devotion which exceeds the rules of the Mafia, you often employ a double standard when it comes to your own behaviour. You think you're being emotionally loyal to your loved one if you sleep with someone else, as long as it's only for sex. Of all the signs, only you can separate your emotions from your sexuality and come out a winner.

However, what about the year ahead?

Well, Venus is the planet of love and it's also the ruler of the partnership area of your chart, so let's see what it's up to this year.

Venus will be squatting in Capricorn up until 18 January. That's the area of your chart devoted to the mind, but also to short journeys, so there's a possibility of meeting new people whilst moving from place to place – stay alert.

From 19 January to 11 February, Venus can be found in Aquarius, the area of your chart devoted to home and family, so it's unlikely that you'll feel like being too gregarious. Instead, your creative talents will be applied to improving your surroundings.

From 12 February to 7 March, Venus can be located in Pisces. Good news, because Pisces is the area of your chart

Love and Sex Year

devoted to fun, socializing and romance, as well as matters related to children. All these sides to life have a happy glow about them, so push ahead.

From 8 to 31 March, Venus can be found in Aries, so there's a happy glow over work matters. If you are an artist you'll be doing very well. From a romantic viewpoint you may be meeting someone special through your job, so stay alert.

From 1 to 25 April, Venus is located in Taurus, your opposite number, throwing a happy glow over all existing relationships. If you have been with the same partner for some considerable while, it's not inconceivable that you might decide to become engaged or even married, and if you do so at this time you've done the right thing.

From 26 April to 20 May, Venus is in Gemini and because of this, those of you involved in big business are likely to have the most romantic time, meeting somebody in connection with your job, or while you're wheeling and dealing.

From 21 May to 14 June, Venus will be occupied in Cancer. There's a suggestion here of romance being found in connection with a foreigner, or whilst travelling abroad.

From 15 June to 10 July, Venus will be in the fiery sign of Leo and that's the zenith point of your chart. Romance could be found through your job and perhaps people at work will make interesting introductions.

From 11 July to 6 August, Venus is in Virgo and this emphasizes a lot of fun in connection with friends, or within team effort. Team mates, acquaintances and friends could be making promising introductions, so if you're single don't turn them down.

From 7 August to 7 September, Venus is in Libra, so you need to take care here, Scorpio, because this suggests that there's a lot going on in secret and behind the scenes. If you are married, you may be tempted to stray, but if you do so, be warned – you will be found out!

From 8 September through to the end of the year, Venus is in your sign, which doesn't seem to be quite fair. The other signs experience the placing of Venus for a few weeks, you've got this for a few months and you are looking good, feeling good and if you have decided to become married or engaged, you have been very clever indeed. But even if not, you're spoiled for choice; the planets are certainly on your side in this area of life, so get out there and enjoy yourself.

Health and Diet Year

It hardly needs saying that between the dates of Scorpio you have the Sun in your sign. Therefore, when the planets are acting up, you could suffer from a deficiency in cell salt, namely Calcium Sulphate, which is commonly known as Plaster of Paris.

This cell salt helps to eradicate accumulations of decaying organic matter, stopping it from lying dormant in the system and injuring the surrounding tissues.

A deficiency of this salt can cause catarrh, lung troubles, boils, ulcers, carbuncles, abscesses and disorders of the liver and kidneys.

If any of these problems occur, supplements of Calcium can be taken in tablet form, or if you know the right foods which contain this substance then pile them on to your plate.

Because you must bottle up your mind in the confines of your body, tension often tyrannizes your energies. But plenty of physical exercise will loosen constricted places and allow your mental processes more freedom.

Tennis is an ideal way to focus mental energies into physical outlet; if you can't make it onto the courts, try jogging, skipping, or running on the spot.

Visualize your anger flowing from your brain, down your spine, into the soles of your feet, and with each movement feel it leaving your body.

Whenever your mind is emotionally charged, it tends to work overtime, and your obsessions can become a demon that destroys a good night's sleep. Learn how to let go and not to be a victim of your own energies. Try yoga for total relaxation.

Meditation will get your mind moving on a slower frequency, so that you will no longer be a slave to your own thoughts.

Since you are prone to extremes and excesses, you often overextend yourself in indulgences of a sybaritic sort. Too much drinking, food, drugs, smoking and sex coupled with too little sleep are guaranteed to be both ageing and anxiety producing. You were the inventor of 'divine decadence' and also the progenitor of degenerative diseases. Since you like to push each experience to the limits, it's a good idea to know just what yours are before you wake up in a strange bed behind bars.

The foods most suitable for you include savoy cabbage, red beet, watercress, prunes, and kale. Milk is one of the best balanced foods, because of its calcium content, and cottage cheese is similarly valuable. Onions are a perfect antiseptic and eliminator and are of great service in the treatment of colds, catarrh, and congestion. Herbs are beneficial to Scorpio and they include sarsaparilla, blue flag, soapwort, yellow dock, marigold, wormwood and horseradish.

However, what about the general pitfalls for the year ahead?

Well, from 1 to 18 January Mars wil be coasting through the watery sign of Pisces, so the outlook is quite good for you

Health and Diet Year

unless you have to travel a great deal. If you do, then take things slowly and methodically or you may run into problems.

On 19 January, Mars will be in Aries and that's the health area of your chart, so you must watch out for minor accidents, especially where hot and sharp objects are concerned. Food poisoning is another health hazard which is easy to avoid, especially if you know what you're allergic to.

From 2 March to 13 April, Mars will be in your opposite sign of Taurus, so once more we have dangers from hot and sharp objects and poisoning. Stay away from people who are germ-laden as you will easily pick up infections at this time.

From 14 April to 27 May, Mars is situated in Gemini, a time when you'll be extremely accident prone. The best way to protect yourself is to take extra care on the roads because if you fail to do so it could be expensive, as well as dangerous to you.

From 28 May to 13 July, Mars will be in Cancer and that's the area of your chart devoted to matters related to abroad and to study. So physically, while on the move, you must take care. Mentally, try not to take on too much; you know exactly when this is happening, but you don't always listen.

From 14 July to 29 August, Mars will be in Leo and that's the area of your chart devoted to work and career, which seems to be causing you a certain amount of stress and aggravation. Try to stay calm and don't let other people 'wind you up'.

From 30 August to 15 October Mars will be in Virgo, so stresses and strains will be coming through team effort and also through your friends and acquaintances. Luckily, you are able to detach yourself whenever you think other people's demands are excessive and that's exactly what you should do during this time.

From 16 October to 1 December, Mars will be in Libra, a rather secretive area of your chart, so any illnesses may not be apparent straightaway. However, if you pamper yourself a bit nothing will develop, with any luck.

From 2 December to the end of month, Mars is in your sign, so you must, once again, watch out for sharp objects and all things that are hot. Fortunately, as a Scorpio, you're a pretty determined character, you don't like the idea of being swept around by the vagaries of astrology or anything else for that matter, so take your life in your hands and you should be able to maintain a healthy and happy year.

Numerology Year

In order to discover the number of any year you are interested in, your 'individual year number', first take your birth date, day and month, and add this to the year you are interested in, be it in the past or in the future. As an example, say you were born on 13 August and the year you are interested in is 2002:

```
  13
+  8
+2002
 2023
```

Then, write down 2 + 0 + 2 + 3 and you will discover this equals 7. This means that your year number is 7. If the number adds up to more than 9, add these two digits together.

You can experiment with this method by taking any year from your past and following this guide to find whether or not numerology works out for you.

The guide is perennial and applicable to all Sun signs: you can look up years for your friends as well as for yourself. Use it to discover general trends ahead, the way you should be

Individual Year Number 1

General Feel
A time for being more self-sufficient and one when you should be ready to really go for it. All opportunities must be snapped up, after careful consideration. Also an excellent time for laying down the foundations for future success in all areas.

Definition
Because this is the number 1 individual year, you will have the chance to start again in many areas of life. The emphasis will be upon the new; there will be fresh faces in your life, more opportunities and perhaps even new experiences. If you were born on either the 1st, 19th or 28th and were born under the sign of Aries or Leo then this will be an extremely important time. It is crucial during this cycle that you are prepared to go it alone, push back horizons and generally open up your mind. Time also for playing the leader or pioneer wherever necessary. If you have a hobby that you wish to turn into a business, or maybe you simply wish to introduce other people to your ideas and plans, then do so whilst experiencing this individual cycle. A great period too for laying down plans for long-term future gains. Therefore, make sure you do your homework well and you will reap the rewards at a later date.

Relationships
This is an ideal period for forming new bonds, perhaps business relationships, new friends and new loves too. You will be

Numerology Year

attracted to those in high positions and with strong personalities. There may also be an emphasis on bonding with people a good deal younger than yourself. If you are already in a long-standing relationship, then it is time to clear away the dead wood between you which may have been causing misunderstandings and unhappiness. Whether in love or business, you will find those who are born under the sign of Aries, Leo or Aquarius far more common in your life, also those born on the following dates: 1st, 4th, 9th, 10th, 13th, 18th, 19th, 22nd and 28th. The most important months for this individual year, when you are likely to meet up with those who have a strong influence on you, are January, May, July and October.

Career

It is likely that you have been wanting to break free and to explore fresh horizons in your career and this is definitely a year for doing so. Because you are in a fighting mood, and because your decision-making qualities as well as your leadership qualities are foremost, it will be an easy matter for you to find assistance as well as to impress other people. Major professional changes are likely and you will also feel more independent within your existing job. Should you want times for making important career moves, then choose Mondays or Tuesdays. These are good days for pushing your luck and presenting your ideas well. Changes connected with your career are going to be more likely during April, May, July and September.

Health

If you have forgotten the name of your doctor or dentist, then this is the year to start regular checkups. A time too when people of a certain age are likely to start wearing glasses. The emphasis seems to be on the eyes. Start a good health regime. This will help you cope with any adverse events that almost assuredly lie ahead. The important months for your own health as well as for loved ones are March, May and August.

Individual Year Number 2

General Feel
You will find it far easier to relate to other people.

Definition
What you will need during this cycle is diplomacy, cooperation and the ability to put yourself in someone else's shoes. Whatever you began last year will now begin to show signs of progress. However, don't expect miracles; changes are going to be slow rather than at the speed of light. Changes will be taking place all around you. It is possible too that you will be considering moving from one area to another, maybe even to another country. There is a lively feel about domesticity and in relationships with the opposite sex too. This is going to be a marvellous year for making things come true and asking for favours. However, on no account should you force yourself and your opinions on other people. A spoonful of honey is going to get you a good deal further than a spoonful of vinegar. If you are born under the sign of Cancer or Taurus, or if your birthday falls on the 2nd, 11th, 20th or 29th, then this year is going to be full of major events.

Relationships
You need to associate with other people far more than is usually the case – perhaps out of necessity. The emphasis is on love, friendship and professional partnerships. The opposite

sex will be much more prepared to get involved in your life than is normally the case. This year you have a far greater chance of becoming engaged or married, and there is likely to be a lovely addition both to your family and to the families of your friends and those closest to you. The instinctive and caring side to your personality is going to be strong and very obvious. You will quickly discover that you will be particularly touchy and sensitive to things that other people say. Further, you will find those born under the sign of Cancer, Taurus and Libra entering your life far more than is usually the case. This also applies to those who are born on the 2nd, 6th, 7th, 11th, 15th, 20th, 24th, 25th or 29th of the month.

Romantic and family events are likely to be emphasized during April, June and September.

Career

There is a strong theme of change here, but there is no point in having a panic attack about that because, after all, life is about change. However, in this particular individual year any transformation or upheaval is likely to be of an internal nature, such as at your place of work, rather than external. You may find your company is moving from one area to another, or perhaps there are changes between departments. Quite obviously then, the most important thing for you to do in order to make your life easy is to be adaptable. There is a strong possibility too that you may be given added responsibility. Do not flinch as this will bring in extra reward.

If you are thinking of searching for employment this year, then try to arrange all meetings and negotiations on Monday and Friday. These are good days for asking for favours or rises too. The best months are March, April, June, August, and December. All these are important times for change.

Health

This individual cycle emphasizes stomach problems. The important thing for you is to eat sensibly, rather than go on a crash diet, for example – this could be detrimental. If you are female then you would be wise to have a checkup at least once during the year ahead just to be sure you can continue to enjoy good health. All should be discriminating when dining out. Check cutlery, and take care that food has not been partially cooked. Furthermore, emotional stress could get you down, but only if you allow it. Provided you set aside some periods of relaxation in each day when you can close your eyes and let everything drift away, you will have little to worry about. When it comes to diet, be sure that the emphasis is on nutrition, rather than fighting the flab. Perhaps it would be a good idea to become less weight conscious during this period and let your body find its natural ideal weight on its own. The months of February, April, July and November may show health changes in some way. Common sense is your best guide during this year.

Individual Year Number 3

General Feel

You are going to be at your most creative and imaginative during this time. There is a theme of expansion and growth and you will want to polish up your self-image in order to make the 'big impression'.

Definition

It is a good year for reaching out, for expansion. Social and artistic developments should be interesting as well as profitable and this will help to promote happiness. There will be a strong urge in you to improve yourself – either your image or your reputation or, perhaps, your mind. Your popularity soars through the ceiling and this delights you. Involving yourself with something creative brings increased success plus a good deal of satisfaction. However, it is imperative that you keep yourself in a positive mood. This will attract attention and appreciation of all your talents. Projects which were begun two years ago are likely to be bearing fruit this year. If you are born under the sign of Pisces or Sagittarius, or your birthday falls on the 3rd, 12th, 21st or 30th, then this year is going to be particularly special and successful.

Relationships

There is a happy-go-lucky feel about all your relationships and you are in a flirty, fancy-free mood. Heaven help anyone trying to catch you during the next twelve months: they will need to get their skates on. Relationships are likely to be light-hearted and fun rather than heavy going. It is possible too that you will find yourself with those who are younger than you, particularly those born under the signs of Pisces and Sagittarius, and those whose birth dates add up to 3, 6 or 9. Your individual cycle shows important months for relationships are March, May, August and December.

Career

As I discussed earlier, this individual number is one that suggests branching out and personal growth, so be ready to take on anything new. Not surprisingly, your career prospects look bright and shiny. You are definitely going to be more ambitious and must keep up that positive façade and attract opportunities. Avoid taking obligations too lightly; it is important that you adopt a conscientious approach to all your responsibilities. You may take on a fresh course of learning or look for a new job, and the important days for doing so would be on Thursday and Friday: these are definitely your best days. This is particularly true in the months of February, March, May, July and November: expect expansion in your life and take a chance during these times.

Health

Because you are likely to be out and about painting the town all the colours of the rainbow, it is likely that health problems could come through over-indulgence or perhaps tiredness. However, if you must have some health problems, I suppose these are the best ones to experience, because they are under your control. There is also a possibility that you may get a little fraught over work, which may result in some emotional scenes. However, you are sensible enough to realize they should not be taken too seriously. If you are prone to skin allergies, then these too could be giving you problems during this particular year. The best advice you can follow is not to go to extremes that will affect your body or your mind. It is all very well to have fun, but after a while too much of it affects not only your health but also the degree of enjoyment you experience. Take extra care between January and March, and June and October, especially where these are winter months for you.

Individual Year Number 4

General Feel

It is back to basics this year. Do not build on shaky foundations. Get yourself organized and be prepared to work a little harder than you usually do and you will come through without any great difficulty.

Definition

It is imperative that you have a grand plan. Do not simply rush off without considering the consequences and avoid dabbling of any kind. It is likely too that you will be gathering more responsibility and on occasions this could lead you to feeling unappreciated, claustrophobic and perhaps overburdened in some ways. Although it is true to say that this cycle in your individual life tends to bring about a certain amount of limitation, whether this be on the personal, the psychological or the financial side of life, you now have the chance to get yourself together and to build on more solid foundations. Security is definitely your key word at this time. When it comes to any project, job or plan, it is important that you ask the right questions. In other words, do your homework and do not rush blindly into anything. That would be a disaster. If you are an Aquarius, a Leo or a Gemini or you are born on the 4th, 13th, 22nd, or the 31st of any month, this individual year will be extremely important and long remembered.

Relationships

You will find that it is the eccentric, the unusual, the unconventional and the downright odd that will be drawn into your life during this particular cycle. It is also strongly possible that people you have not met for some time may be re-entering your circle and an older person or somebody outside your own social or perhaps religious background will be drawn to you too. When it comes to the romantic side of life, again you are drawn to that which is different from usual. You may even form a relationship with someone who comes from a totally different background, perhaps from far away. Something unusual about them stimulates and excites you. Gemini, Leo and Aquarius are your likely favourites, as well as anyone whose birth number adds up to 1, 4, 5 or 7. Certainly the most exciting months for romance are going to be February, April, July and November. Make sure then that you socialize a lot during these particular times, and be ready for literally anything.

Career

Once more we have the theme of the unusual and different in this area of life. You may be plodding along in the same old rut when suddenly lightning strikes and you find yourself besieged by offers from other people and, in a panic, not quite sure what to do. There may be a period when nothing particular seems to be going on when, to your astonishment, you are given a promotion or some exciting challenge. Literally anything can happen in this particular cycle of your life. The individual year 4 also inclines towards added responsibilities and it is important that you do not off-load them onto other people or cringe in fear. They will eventually pay off and in the meantime you will be gaining in experience and paving the way for greater success in the future. When you want to arrange any kind of meeting, negotiation or perhaps ask for a favour at work, then try to do so on a Monday or a Wednesday for the luckiest results. January, February, April, October and November are certainly the months when you must play the opportunist and be ready to say yes to anything that comes your way.

Health

The biggest problems that you will have to face this year are caused by stress, so it is important that you attend to your diet and take life as philosophically as possible, as well as being ready to adapt to changing conditions. You are likely to find that people you thought you knew well are acting out of character and this throws you off balance. Take care, too, when visiting the doctor. Remember that you are dealing with a human being and that doctors, like the rest of us, can make mistakes. Unless you are 100 per cent satisfied then go for a second opinion over anything important. Try to be sceptical about yourself because you are going to be a good deal more moody than usual. The times that need special attention are February, May, September and November. If any of these months fall in the winter part of your year, then wrap up well and dose up on vitamin C.

Individual Year Number 5

General Feel
There will be many more opportunities for you to get out and about, and travel is certainly going to be playing a large part in your year. Change, too, must be expected and even embraced – after all, it is part of life. You will have more free time and choices, so all in all things look promising.

Definition
It is possible that you tried previously to get something off the launchpad, but for one reason or another it simply didn't happen. Luckily, you now get a chance to renew those old plans and put them into action. You are certainly going to feel that things are changing for the better in all areas. You will be more actively involved with the public and enjoy a certain amount of attention and publicity. You may have failed in the past but this year mistakes will be easier to accept and learn from; you are going to find yourself both physically and mentally more in tune with your environment and with those you

care about than ever before. If you are a Gemini or a Virgo or are born on the 5th, 14th or 23rd, then this is going to be a period of major importance for you and you must be ready to take advantage of this.

Relationships
Lucky you! Your sexual magnetism goes through the ceiling and you will be involved in many relationships during the year ahead. You have that extra charisma about you which will be attracting others and you can look forward to being choosy. There will be an inclination to be drawn to those who are considerably younger than yourself. It is likely too that you will find that those born under the signs of Taurus, Gemini, Virgo and Libra as well as those whose birth date adds up to 2, 5 or 6 will play an important part in your year. The months for attracting others in a big way are January, March, June, October and December.

Career
This is considered by all numerologists as being one of the best numbers for self-improvement in all areas, but particularly on the professional front. It will be relatively easy for you to sell your ideas and yourself, as well as to push your skills and expertise under the noses of other people. They will certainly sit up and take notice. Clearly, then, this is a time for you to view the world as your oyster and to get out there and grab your piece of the action. You have increased confidence and should be able to get exactly what you want. Friday and Wednesday are perhaps the best days if looking for a job or going to negotiations or interviews, or in fact for generally pushing yourself into the limelight. Watch out for March, May, September, October or December. Something of great

importance could pop up at this time. There will certainly be a chance for advancement; whether you take it or not is, of course, entirely up to you.

Health

Getting a good night's rest could be your problem during the year ahead, since that mind of yours is positively buzzing and won't let you rest. Try turning your brain off at bedtime, otherwise you will finish up irritable and exhausted. Try to take things a step at a time without rushing around. Meditation may help you to relax and do more for your physical wellbeing than anything else. Because this is an extremely active year, you will need to do some careful planning so that you can cope with ease rather than rushing around like a demented mayfly. Furthermore, try to avoid going over the top with alcohol, food, sex, gambling or anything which could be described as a 'quick fix'. During January, April, August and October, watch yourself a bit, you could do with some pampering, particularly if these happen to be winter months for you.

Individual Year Number 6

General Feel

There is likely to be increased responsibility and activity within your domestic life. There will be many occasions when you will be helping loved ones and your sense of duty is going to be strong.

Definition

Activities for the most part are likely to be centred around property, family, loved ones, romance and your home. Your artistic appreciation will be good and you will be drawn to anything that is colourful and beautiful, and possessions that have a strong appeal to your eye or even your ear. Where domesticity is concerned, there is a strong suggestion that you may move out of one home into another. This is an excellent time, too, for self-education, for branching out, for graduating, for taking on some extra courses – whether simply to improve your appearance or to improve your mind. When it comes to your social life you are inundated with chances to attend events. You are going to be a real social butterfly, flitting from scene to scene and enjoying yourself thoroughly. Try to accept nine out of ten invitations that come your way because they bring with them chances of advancement. If you are born on the 6th, 15th or 24th, or should your birth sign be Taurus, Libra or Cancer, then this year will be long remembered as a very positive one.

Relationships

When it comes to love, sex and romance the individual year 6 is perhaps the most successful. It is a time for being swept off your feet, for becoming engaged or even getting married. On the more negative side, perhaps, there could be separation and divorce. However, the latter can be avoided, provided you are prepared to sit down and communicate properly. There is an emphasis too on pregnancy and birth, or changes in existing relationships. Circumstances will be sweeping you along. If you are born under the sign of Taurus, Cancer or Libra, then it is even more likely that this will be a major year for you, as well as for those born on dates adding up to 6, 3 or 2. The most memorable months of your year are going to be February, May, September and November. Grab all opportunities to enjoy yourself and improve your relationships during these periods.

Career

A good year for this side of life too, with the chances of promotion and recognition for past efforts all coming your way. You will be able to improve your position in life even though it is likely that recently you have been disappointed. On the cash front, big rewards will come flooding in mainly because you are prepared to fulfil your obligations and commitments without complaint or protest. Other people will appreciate all the efforts you have put in, so plod along and you will find your efforts will not have been in vain. Perversely, if you are looking for a job or setting up an interview, negotiation or a meeting, or simply want to advertise your talents in some way, then your best days for doing so are Monday, Thursday and Friday. Long-term opportunities are very strong during the months of February, April, August, September and November. These are the key periods for pushing yourself up the ladder of success.

Health

If you are to experience any problems of a physical nature during this year, then they could be tied up with the throat, nose or the tonsils, plus the upper parts of the body. Basically, what you need to stay healthy during this year is plenty of sunlight, moderate exercise, fresh air and changes of scene. Escape to the coast if this is at all possible. The months for being particularly watchful are March, July, September and December. Think twice before doing anything during these times and there is no reason why you shouldn't stay hale and hearty for the whole year.

Individual Year Number 7

General Feel

A year for inner growth and for finding out what really makes you tick and what you need to make you happy. Self-awareness and discovery are all emphasized during the individual year 7.

Definition

You will be provided with the opportunity to place as much emphasis as possible on your personal life and your own well-being. There will be many occasions when you will find yourself analysing your past motives and actions, and giving more attention to your own personal needs, goals and desires. There will also be many occasions when you will want to escape any kind of confusion, muddle or noise; time spent alone will not be wasted. This will give you the chance to meditate and also to examine exactly where you have come to so far, and where you want to go in the future. It is important you make up your mind what you want out of this particular year because once you have done so you will attain those ambitions. Failure to do this could mean you end up chasing your own tail and that is a pure waste of time and energy. You will also discover that secrets about yourself and other people could be surfacing during this year. If you are born under the sign of Pisces or Cancer, or on the 7th, 16th or 25th of the month, then this year will be especially wonderful.

Relationships

It has to be said from the word go that this is not the best year for romantic interest. A strong need for contemplation will mean spending time on your own. Any romance that does develop this year may not live up to your expectations, but, providing you are prepared to take things as they come without jumping to conclusions, then you will enjoy yourself without getting hurt. Decide exactly what it is you have in mind and then go for it. Romantic interests this year are likely to be with people who are born on dates that add up to 2, 4 or 7, or with people born under the sign of Cancer or Pisces. Watch for romantic opportunities during January, April, August and October.

Career
When we pass through this particular individual cycle, two things in life tend to occur: retirement from the limelight, and a general slowing down, perhaps by taking leave of absence or maybe retraining in some way. It is likely too that you will become more aware of your own occupational expertise and skills – you will begin to understand your true purpose in life and will feel much more enlightened. Long-sought-after goals begin to come to life if you have been drifting of late. The best attitude to have throughout this year is an exploratory one when it comes to your work. If you want to set up negotiations, interviews or meetings, arrange them for Monday or Friday. In fact, any favours you seek should be tackled on these days. January, March, July, August, October and December are particularly good for self-advancement.

Health
Since, in comparison to previous years, this is a rather quiet time, health problems are likely to be minor. Some will possibly come through irritation or worry and the best thing to do is to attempt to remain meditative and calm. This state of mind will bring positive results. Failure to do so may create unnecessary problems by allowing your imagination to run completely out

of control. You need time this year to restore, recuperate and contemplate. Any health changes that do occur are likely to happen in February, June, August and November.

Individual Year Number 8

General Feel
This is going to be a time for success, for making important moves and changes, a time when you may gain power and certainly one when your talents are going to be recognized.

Definition
This individual year gives you the chance to 'think big'; it is a time when you can occupy the limelight and wield power. If you were born on the 8th, 17th or 26th of the month or come under the sign of Capricorn, pay attention to this year and make sure you make the most of it. You should develop greater maturity and discover a true feeling of faith and destiny, both in yourself and in events that occur. This part of the cycle is connected with career, ambition and money, but debts from the past will have to be repaid. For example, an old responsibility or debt that you may have avoided in past years may reappear to haunt you. However, whatever you do with these twelve months, aim high – think big, think success and above all be positive.

Relationships
This particular individual year is one which is strongly connected with birth, divorce and marriage – most of the landmarks we experience in life, in fact. Love-wise, those who are more experienced or older than you, or people of power,

authority, influence or wealth, will be very attractive. This year will be putting you back in touch with those from your past – old friends, comrades, associates, and even romances from long ago crop up once more. You should not experience any great problems romantically this year, especially if you are dealing with Capricorns or Librans, or with those whose date of birth adds up to 8, 6 or 3. The best months for romance to develop are likely to be March, July, September and December.

Career

The number 8 year is generally believed to be the best one when it comes to bringing in cash. It is also good for asking for a rise or achieving promotion or authority over other people. This is your year for basking in the limelight of success, the result perhaps of your past efforts. Now you will be rewarded. Financial success is all but guaranteed, provided you keep faith with your ambitions and yourself. It is important that you set major goals for yourself and work slowly towards them. You will be surprised how easily they are fulfilled. Conversely, if you are looking for work, then do set up interviews, negotiations and meetings, preferably on Saturday, Thursday or Friday, which are your luckiest days. Also watch out for chances to do yourself a bit of good during February, June, July, September and November.

Health

You can avoid most health problems, particularly headaches, constipation or liver problems, by avoiding depression and feelings of loneliness. It is important when these descend that you keep yourself busy enough not to dwell on them. When it comes to receiving attention from the medical profession you would be well advised to get a second opinion. Eat wisely, try to keep a positive and enthusiastic outlook on life and all will be well. Periods which need special care are January, May, July and October. Therefore, if these months fall during the winter part of your year, wrap up well and dose yourself with vitamins.

Individual Year Number 9

General Feel

A time for tying up loose ends. Wishes are likely to be fulfilled and matters brought to swift conclusions. Inspiration runs amok. Much travel is likely.

Definition

The number 9 individual year is perhaps the most successful of all. It tends to represent the completion of matters and affairs, whether in work, business, or personal affairs. Your ability to let go of habits, people and negative circumstances or situations, that may have been holding you back, is strong. The sympathetic and humane side to your character also surfaces and you learn to give more freely of yourself without expecting anything in return. Any good deeds that you do will certainly be well rewarded in terms of satisfaction, and perhaps financially, too. If you are born under the sign of Aries or Scorpio, or on the 9th, 18th or 27th of the month, this is certainly going to be an all-important year.

Relationships

The individual year 9 is a cycle which gives appeal as well as influence. Because of this, you will be getting emotionally tied up with members of the opposite sex who may be outside your usual cultural or ethnic group. The reason for this is that this particular number relates to humanity and of course this tends to quash ignorance, pride and bigotry. You also discover that Aries, Leo and Scorpio people are going to be much more evident in your domestic affairs, as well as those whose birth dates add up to 9, 3 or 1. The important months for relationships are February, June, August and November. These will be extremely hectic and eventful from a romantic viewpoint and there are times when you could be swept off your feet.

Career
This is a year which will help to make many of your dreams and ambitions come true. Furthermore, it is an excellent time for success if you are involved in marketing your skills, talents and expertise more widely. You may be thinking of expanding abroad for example and, if so, this is certainly a good idea. You will find that harmony and cooperation with your fellow workers are easier than before and this will help your dreams and ambitions. The best days for you if you want to line up meetings or negotiations are going to be Tuesdays and Thursdays, and this also applies if you are looking for employment or want a special day for doing something of an ambitious nature. Employment or business changes could also feature during January, May, June, August and October.

Health
The only physical problems you may have during this particular year will be because of accidents, so be careful. Try, too, to avoid unnecessary tension and arguments with other people. Take extra care when you are on the roads: no drinking and driving, for example. You will only have problems if you play your own worst enemy. Be extra careful when in the kitchen or bathroom: sharp instruments that you find in these areas can lead to cuts, unless you take care.

Your Sun Sign Partner

Scorpio Woman with Scorpio Man

This may be love at first sight, but whether the love will be long-lasting depends on the maturity of the two individuals.

Both are intense, jealous, possessive and dominated by pride. She is warm, sensual and often self-sacrificing. He is sexually demanding and definitely ego-oriented. Unless they can meet halfway and make it last, hostilities may brew heavily under the surface.

Although to the outside world he is at best a mystery, to her mind he is like an open book. Unfortunately, what she reads may not always please her.

He wants to be boss, to set down the rules, and may try to take over her life. Since she wants to be securely loved, for a while she'll give in and seethe under the surface. But when the resentment really starts to smoulder, he may find himself in the divorce courts quicker than he can count to one.

If both are moody, it may be a very stormy situation, where suspicions rise and fall as quickly as the tide. After the afternoons of sarcasm come the evenings of passion. Followed by mellow mornings of sensual splendour. Whatever you wish to say about the combination of Scorpio and Scorpio, there are so many emotional ups and downs that things never get a chance to get boring. However, they may get so violent and exhausting that after 24 hours both people feel they have just run the four-minute mile.

If both are more highly involved, this match is an excellent one, where psychotherapy will undoubtedly have a place. Both may be so sensitive to the moods of the other that they over-analyse the other's comments to such an extent that they start dreaming about them. Although there may be many sleepless nights during which one member of this partnership stays up till dawn in an effort to make a simple scene complex, there may also be much sharing based on the mutual desire for personal growth.

In this relationship, togetherness may be taken to such an extreme that the couple start to take on the attributes of Siamese twins. The danger is that one day, one or both may feel the need for separation surgery.

All Scorpios need to understand is that there really is a mid-point between autonomy and total possession. Only when they make a sincere effort to tread that thin line do they relinquish the need to be dominated by their own control.

Scorpio Woman

Scorpio woman with Aries man
He'll sweep you off your feet and carry you over the threshold, and for once, his mind will stop trying to figure out whether you're both going in the right direction. However, since both parties are coming from such opposite places, this passion is short-lived, and in any prolonged involvement you're likely to think of him as selfish and silly.

He'll dazzle you with his courage, vitality and super macho stamina. But when you notice this is a much repeated repertoire and that he's treating you as one of a thousand faces, suddenly the starry eyed passion dwindles.

Scorpio woman with Taurus man

Regardless of what you've heard, he's no delight unless he's cooking you dinner, and he's probably doing that only because he's too cheap to take you out. If you break a tooth on the bread, it's undoubtedly because he bought it on sale. And if the milk in your coffee separates, it's only because he wanted to use up last month's before he opened a new bottle.

He's terribly sensitive – when it comes to his own feelings. But should you desire him to understand your subtle emotional situation, you may have to lean over and shout in his ear. But you shouldn't expect him to understand the first time around, or the fifth, or the tenth, or the sixteenth ...

Scorpio woman with Gemini man

At its best, this combination is friendship. At its worst, it is a quiet but very painful immolation. Although he thinks he's very clever, you sometimes see him as simple-minded. He seems to be going in every direction but getting nowhere, when you stay in the one place but travel very fast.

It's true that his sense of the ludicrous always keeps you laughing, but his constant lateness ignites your Scorpio temper.

Scorpio woman with Cancer man

For you, he's a package deal – a man with the qualities of Mother. He'll understand your moods, kiss you on the forehead, bake you apple pie, and serve you tea with lemon.

This combination is highly compatible, especially if you are born during the last week or so of the Scorpio period.

He'll feel flattered by your jealousy and return the feeling fourfold, which will make you feel all the more secure. You are his constant source of inspiration, and he is your constant bastion of support.

Scorpio woman with Leo man

You'll make him wonder if he's speaking a foreign language that sounds like English. That's when you're communicating. And, as long as you open your mouth, he's always foolish enough to think he actually has a chance of understanding you. But when you close it and stare at his lower lip – forget it. All hope is lost and so is the fleeting sense of his sanity.

Needless to say, the compatibility here is not compelling. And in terms of rapport, it would be easier to just mumble to the cat.

Scorpio woman with Virgo man

Since he's a nervous sort, you had better try not to stare, or else he'll break out in a rash. He's attracted to your depth, your intensity and your sensuality. You appreciate his stability, earthy sexuality and sense of purpose. He may not understand you, and think your emotions silly, but he'll stay up all night listening to your problems. Even if you're repeating your points 25 times and going over the same sentence hour after hour, he will do his best to listen.

Initially, this relationship may kindle a few favourable sparks, but for the most part, you should consider it to be one that you're just passing through. Otherwise, you can expect a lifetime of index cards and multi-vitamins on your birthday.

Scorpio woman with Libra man

One look and you'll have him, but it will be quite some time before he feels secure that he has you.

He is a charmer, but you see through it. Sometimes you think he's superficial and lacking in substance. At other times, you appreciate his sense of romance and the fact that he prefers organ music to rock and roll.

He'll woo you with lilacs, champagne and perfume. If you prepare dinner for him, he'll bring fresh basil for the salad. But when he wins you, it's only with an offer of a lasting relationship.

Give him a lifetime and he'll still never understand you. However, he may desperately fall in love, compliment your cooking and keep referring to a future of connubial bliss. However, you need to make sure that that future is with you before you get too carried away.

Scorpio woman with Sagittarius man

He is a character, and one who is guaranteed to charm you. He has the kind of sense of adventure that can transform a shopping spree into an African safari, and a formal sit-down dinner into a discotheque.

You'll find him funny, friendly and fantastically silly – especially when he takes you to the zoo to introduce you to the orangutan.

Quite unintentionally he has been known to stand up a few damsels in his lifetime. So if he should invite you on a canoe trip that never happens, and you finds that he has taken a last-minute jaunt to Afghanistan, you should take it all in your stride. In this instance, just walking beside him, you feel as if you have to run to keep up.

Scorpio woman with Capricorn man

You admire his ambition, but get lonely when you never see him. He respects your devotion, but at times tends to take it for granted. At worst this relationship can turn into a bitter emotional battle. At best, it can be a situation of mutual respect, much support, and a shared sense of responsibility.

He tends to be depressed, especially when his career is going more slowly than anticipated, because he's only a Corporate Vice President at the age of 28. If you are supportive of his maniacal power drive and listen to his daily problems about how his secretary forgets to dot her 'I's' he will develop the deepest attachment to you. However, you shouldn't expect that in return he will appreciate, tolerate, or understand your moods or your deepest feelings.

Scorpio woman with Aquarius man

He will never forget you, because you are one illusive woman. Regardless of the amount of time he spends with you, he'll feel so close and yet so far, and that is the key to his amorous idealism. He loves your mind, your sexuality and your perception. But your emotions are quite another matter – those he finds interesting only when they don't become confining. He has no idea of where your feelings are coming from or where they are going or what they are really doing there; however, he has a lot of theories.

Scorpio woman with Pisces man

He'll treat you like a drug. The problem is that you are a woman. This irreconcilable fact is the essence of your problem with Mr Pisces.

With regard to sex, this man is a passive sort. With regard

to love, he is a bundle of emotion, and as to romance, he prefers the drug-like dream of your distant approach far more than your personal appearance.

It's true that Mr Pisces is as frail as his fantasies. In a time of crisis, he'll cry on your shoulder, but you shouldn't let this flimflam fool you. When caught in an emotional dead end, he can be cruel, sadistic and cunning.

Although at times he sees himself as mysterious, you can see right through him. Despite what he may think, he never creates anything subtly. He learned it somewhere from a Scorpio. And judging from his behaviour, that's only a fraction of the learning he still has in store.

Scorpio Man

Scorpio man with Aries woman

This combination is passion personified, but one that involves a primitive kind of power struggle in which egos will clash so hard that they both get bruises.

She'll boss you around, and if you don't do as she says, she'll step on your foot. You'll snarl and throw out a few vicious sarcastic comments, but the worst part is that she is so self-centred that she won't even be listening.

Scorpio man with Taurus woman

You'll find her warm, sensual, domestic, insecure and very vulnerable. You can see right through her quiche lorraine, straight into her soul, and what you'll see is a tremendous need to be loved and a longing to be needed.

For Ms Taurus this is a fatal attraction. Her heart will get caught up in your contradictions and you'll enjoy the power you have in just watching her trying to get out. She's like a fly under the foot of a tarantula, and whichever direction she chooses, she's going to get stepped on.

Her greatest desire is for an honest relationship without games, and the kind of passion that comes without pain. You find such scenes comforting only in the dark night of your soul when you feel sad and lonely. At all other times you want her attention to be galvanized by some sort of challenge. In the long run you'll only leave Ms Taurus feeling cold and hungry.

Therefore, the outcome of this meeting is most likely to be two people who pass in the night. If she's smart, the first thing she should do is keep walking. In this way she'll save herself a lot of heartache, and you'll save yourself a few inches off your waistline from her cooking.

Scorpio man with Gemini woman

She'll play havoc with your emotions and when you act moody and macabre just to scare her, she'll giggle in your face and chatter on as if she didn't see you.

There's no way you can control her, because she's a law unto herself. If you bombard her with your mysterious airs then she'll grin, telling you, 'you can't be serious'. You are flip, funny and always have the last word. If you attack her with savage sarcasm then she'll smile and get back with instantaneous retort.

At first you'll find this woman refreshing, but after your energies have had a chance to blend, it's likely that you'll both need a psychic purge.

Scorpio man with Cancer woman

She'll nurture your needs, make you fat and happy on her cooking and try to be understanding when you're being surly.

You are kind, giving, compassionate and more sympathetic than a Red Cross nurse.

All she needs in return is your love. She wants to be smothered in it. She wants to be drowned. She needs to be possessed, cherished and suffocated in order to feel secure. She wants to hold you, consume you, devour you and digest you, and what will remain, remains to be seen.

This could be a great match, should you be ready to settle for some connubial bliss. However, should you have only a good fling in mind, after she tells you her Sun sign, you should keep on walking.

Scorpio man with Leo woman

If there are no water signs on her own personal chart, this meeting will start off like a lusty Italian movie and terminate like a French film where nothing really happens and even the characters are so bored they walk away.

You are a mystery even to yourself. At least if she has some Scorpio in her chart, emotionally she'll understand you, because you'll both be starting from the same place – total obscurity.

When you communicate in convolutions of thought and feeling, feeling and thought, feeling and feeling, then thought and thought – because it's easier than just feeling, she'll either tell you you're boring her or inform you she's just remembered that she has another date.

Scorpio man with Virgo woman

At first she may seem cold, but in fact she's just fragile. You will appreciate her mind and her stability. Together you can have a companionship that is quiet and comfortable. The problem is that you desire one that is noisy and intense.

Here there's a lot of talk but very little action, and passion simply does not reign supreme. Together you can analyse your feelings until you both fall asleep, but it is highly unlikely that you can get the matter to reign over the mind. All the women in your life who have forced you to passivity did it through sheer sensual impact; niceness was never a consideration. That is why, rather than getting involved with you, Ms Virgo is far better off with her pet turtle. You'll always be looking for what isn't there, but a turtle just looks and looks!

Scorpio man with Libra woman

She'll give you a sense of balance, and in return, you'll give her a taste of intense love. You have a special sense of the beautiful and can create a setting of the most seductive creature comforts.

You'll appreciate her good sense of humour and the fact that she is airy and easy to be with. She'll clear away your murky moods and fill your life with the little loving acts that take your heart away.

She is sensual and loving, while you are sexual and possessive. But despite her suspicions, she is everything you want and need. The questions is: are you everything she wants and needs? Since her needs overtake her desires, she'll be able to settle and make herself enjoy it.

Scorpio man with Sagittarius woman

The Sagittarius lady loves to laugh and just wishes that you did. If you stick around long enough she'll be willing to teach you. Despite personality differences, she is wise, positive and philosophical, and has the energy and enthusiasm that overwhelms you.

She is athletic and daring and could spend the entire day playing tennis in 100° while her enthusiasm will keep you on the court until after sundown.

Her wisdom will force you to travel in different directions, and her optimism will encourage your growth. She will help you to rise to the heights and share your revelations once you've both returned. Together you could take each other to a place that the other has never been to, and all through this a deepening love will generate as you realize even greater joy.

Scorpio man with Capricorn woman
In this relationship there's a lot of talk but very little emotional understanding. However, in many ways the attraction is so irresistible that it borders on being fatal. From the very start she will be bewitched and you will be turned on. The ensuing situation could be definitely erotic, but in the long run emotionally deadening.

Your behaviour will puzzle her, pain her and put her into an emotional place where she starts doubting herself. The danger comes when she begins to believe that she deserves what little you give her. At this point, she should either withdraw or confront the fact that she's looking for misery.

Scorpio man with Aquarius woman
You'll want to make love, but she'll want to go to the movies. When you are making love, she'll be musing over why the film ended without music.

You'll need to forget about controlling her – she's so detached that she'll end up controlling you through your obsession with controlling her!

She's so easy to be with that in a peculiar way you find her irresistible. She's like a breath of fresh air, but if you stay around her too long, you might start to feel cold. You are passion personified, while she is mental and remote. You embrace direct experience while she prefers having hers vicariously. After ten years together you may tell her you want an open marriage and she'll tell you she thought it always was.

Scorpio man with Pisces woman

Sexually this combination is so powerful that both may end up on the floor. She'll control you through her desire and you'll devour her through your control. Both could expire through sheer exhaustion of the situation, but what a lovely way to go. As this kind of physical chemistry is narcotic, you should expect to get hooked. When you are together, it may come to the point where you stop eating, sleeping and thinking, and start losing weight. However, just how many banana cherry splits can we possibly eat?

Your moods drag her down and her dependence irritates. You like your emotions to be challenged, while she likes hers to be gratified. You like a woman who is ambitious, self-possessed and successful. She's looking for a man who is all of the above so that she can be taken care of. Much depends on other influences on the birth chart – naturally this partnership can be made to work and when it does it can be fantastic. However, for the majority of the time it's very much a love/hate affair that's likely to be memorable.

Monthly and Daily Guides

JANUARY

The Sun will be diggings its way through Capricorn up until 20 January, and that's the area of your chart devoted to sales, the affairs of brothers and sisters and short journeys, all of which should be extremely successful, so don't hesitate to say 'yes' when you're asked to do any of these.

On 20 January, the Sun will be moving into Aquarius, the area of your chart devoted to home, property and family, so you're going to become something of a home body. You'll also feel really creative right now so this would be a good time to get on with home improvements or other projects you have been putting off.

Mercury will also be in Aquarius from 4 January, and you will suddenly feel the need to spruce up your surroundings. Mind you, you probably haven't even got around to getting rid of the Christmas decorations yet, so no wonder the whole place is looking a bit sad. It's definitely a time for a new broom to sweep your life clean, both mentally, physically and any other way you can think of.

Monthly and Daily Guides: January

Venus will be squatting in Capricorn until 18 January and there seems to be quite a lot of buying and selling going on. Maybe you're visiting the sales and getting things at a cheap price – that always appeals to you, doesn't it?

On 19 January, Venus will be moving on into Aquarius and that's the area of your chart devoted to the home, so there may be a lot of peace, harmony and closeness at home. Of course, this is always nice and you will be making the most of it – and why shouldn't you?

Mars will be in Pisces until 18 January, and that's the area of your chart devoted to sports, children and the good times. Mind you, offspring could be a little boisterous at this time and you may have to calm them down; there's a reason for this, but only you know that. However, don't be too brisk with them otherwise you'll be falling out with your partner and you don't need that. On 19 January Mars will be moving into the fiery sign of Aries and this indicates that you may be accident-prone and should avoid taking risks. Be aware of danger areas in the home, particularly the kitchen and bathroom.

The pattern made by the stars seems to suggest that most of your activity will be connected with home, family and maybe romance. Where the latter is concerned, if you happen to be fancy free, make sure you're looking good and feeling great, and go out where you can bask in the limelight – that's where you ought to be at this time, so don't make any mistake about it.

All in all, this isn't a bad January. It's not a month any of us really enjoy but, for you, you could fare a lot better than other people, so don't knock it.

1 TUESDAY There's a chance of reconciliation today if you and your partner are prepared to put your differences to one side. However, it doesn't help that a sexy friend is attracted to you. It will do wonders for your ego, but not a lot for the state of your relationship. Whatever you do, keep feelings to yourself and a mutual attraction a secret. As far as making plans is concerned, you are at your most creative and ingenious.

2 WEDNESDAY This could be the beginning of an extraordinary period when miracles may well happen. Whatever or whoever you've been fantasizing about, now is the time to turn these dreams into reality. Anything's possible – all you have to do is believe and the rest will follow as if by magic. If you're out socializing, look your best as you'll be whisked away to some glamorous gathering. This particular day and the next are probably as good as it's going to get for a while.

3 THURSDAY You can be successful in your chosen career as long as you follow your intuition and keep one or two aces up your sleeve. Getting on the right side of people of influence will also be great for your reputation. However, it seems you're not yet ready to make the most significant move: this will decide your fate one way or another. Enjoy the sensation of drifting through life – it won't last much longer.

4 FRIDAY Today Mercury will be moving into Aquarius and that's the area of your chart devoted to home and family. If you are thinking about moving, this is the time to step up your efforts. For those already settled, it's a period for entertaining; your home is going to resemble a railway station, but you'll be enjoying all of the activity – nothing to worry about there.

5 SATURDAY The promise of a relationship brings will excite you more than the reality. But whether you're lost in a fantasy world or spending a lot of time in the bedroom, sex and imagination go hand in hand. Back out in the big wide world, you're gearing up to something special. It may be a holiday with friends, a course in a subject that fascinates, or a group event where you'll have the chance to speak up for what you believe in.

6 SUNDAY Anyone who attempts to stand in your way is sure to find their foolish action is short lived as well as unsuccessful. Right now the majority of your efforts and energies are directed to breaking down barriers that still exist between workmates and contacts. Be open-minded and prepared to receive sympathy and support whenever or wherever it's offered.

7 MONDAY Today, Venus and Jupiter are in aspect and this seems to suggest a certain amount of luck where money is concerned, but also a certain amount of waste. Furthermore, other people are in a like-minded mood; if it happens to be your mate then this could be an expensive time. Trim down your outgoings and try to conserve, otherwise you'll be in trouble at a later date.

8 TUESDAY You're going places in your career and the more creative your work and activities, the more successful you'll be. But hold back your fantastic ideas for one more week as the time's not right to divulge them, and you want to surprise everyone. In love, you may feel romantically towards someone you've met fairly recently. However, their interest is in sex rather than love, and this will become painfully obvious over the next few days or so.

♏

9 WEDNESDAY You're perfectly in tune with the spirit of the time and whatever you begin right now will work like magic. Trust yourself and get involved in new technology, new trends and exciting developments in any area of life. Whether you're on holiday, surfing the internet, or brushing up your qualifications, you've never been happier. Take note, because this means you may have touched on your true vocation.

10 THURSDAY Passion and romance go hand in hand and you can't fail to feel dizzy in love. A new relationship will offer you unusual and unexpected experiences and, this time around, you're willing to go with it. However, it is stability you crave and giving up the steady option in order to ride a rollercoaster of emotional highs and lows can work only for so long. Enjoy the love affair while it lasts, but don't give it your heart, soul and body.

11 FRIDAY Work and being of service to others are your true passions, but even you will want to cut back so that you can spend time with someone special. You may be in the grip of a powerful attraction with a compelling person you met through work. One of you will make a declaration of love.

12 SATURDAY To all appearances you seem confident and optimistic as ever, but on the inside, you're feelings seem to be churned around. No wonder, because it's likely that you have been bottling them up for some while recently, and now is the time when you can no longer do so. Mind you, save your outbursts for when you leave work, because colleagues seem determined to take everything you do or say the wrong way, so at least during the daytime the best course of action is to do as little as possible and then let yourself go in the evening.

Monthly and Daily Guides: January

13 SUNDAY Today is the day of the new Moon and it occurs in the earthy sign of Capricorn. That's the area of your chart devoted to buying and selling and the affairs of brothers and sisters, which isn't bad because if you're the type of person who likes to get something for nothing, which I'm sure you are, then you'll be out doing your best to do just that. Furthermore, you seem to be in the spotlight for one reason or another, but don't knock it.

14 MONDAY This is not a day for taking unnecessary gambles; in fact, your best plan by far is to stick to the rules and make certain you do nothing to rock the boat. You may feel a little isolated but there are still some people you can trust. As long as they are approached in the right way, they will be very happy to pass on some useful and valuable information to you.

15 TUESDAY You may be in something of a fighting mood, but remember there's always somebody who is either in a better position, or more important or stronger and better connected than you, so don't start a disagreement unless you stand a pretty good chance of winning. Better still, get someone in an influential position to back you up and then you can't possibly go wrong – or can you?

16 WEDNESDAY Today, clear thinking is not likely to be on the agenda. You will need to double check your social arrangements and your work because it will be far too easy for you to make errors and this, in turn, will lead to frustration when you have to redo work or even make a complete turn around. Check out your diary and make sure you know exactly where you're supposed to be and at what time, because if you keep people hanging around they won't be best pleased.

♏

17 THURSDAY The stars today are advising you to rely on your hunches and imagination as well as intuition. The problem is, of course, can you turn off your active head? Hopefully you can, because this is a way to find success, so see what you can do. This evening avoid any gossip which is going around because you'll be tempted to elaborate and then you'll find yourself in trouble.

18 FRIDAY Today Mercury decides to go into retrograde movement. Mercury rules the area of your chart devoted to friends and acquaintances and so other people may be downright awkward. Never mind, you can always test the water and ask them for a small favour and if they explode then you know to leave them well alone for the time being.

19 SATURDAY Today, to your surprise, you may find that bosses or colleagues are openly against your plans and objectives. Even so, having tried to explain what you're attempting to achieve, you must push on. The more determined you are to stick to your ambitions and dreams, the more likely you are to achieve them. You do enjoy a challenge from time to time and nothing will give you greater pleasure than to prove other people wrong.

20 SUNDAY Today the stars suggest that by paying attention to small details you can find success. In actual fact, if you let your mind stray even for a moment, you could miss out on something of great importance. Furthermore, you can learn as much from a colleague or a partner's mistakes as you would from your own, but fortunately with none of the embarrassment or pain which usually follows.

♏

Monthly and Daily Guides: January

21 MONDAY Personal or domestic affairs appear to be under something of a cloud and it doesn't matter what you say or do, nothing will restore the peace. Do your best not to get rattled and be assured that other people, especially loved ones, will soon come around to your way of thinking. It would be a good idea to side-step any kind of showdown for the time being, but you should be provided with an opportunity to clear the air a little later on.

22 TUESDAY Concentration may break down at any moment, and situations which can normally be controlled with one hand tied behind your back seem to overwhelm you. The best thing to do at this time is to occupy yourself with trivia, make plans for the future, but avoid making any major moves. You're also advised to check on your social calendar this evening because other people may have changed their minds.

23 WEDNESDAY You'll need to be careful when dealing with anything international, or connected with travel, as unnecessary difficulties will crop up unless you check. You may also find learning new skills a problem unless you do some double checking. Be patient with yourself because you most certainly need some of this precious commodity, which sadly you often lack.

24 THURSDAY You should take nothing for granted at this time in life. Creative work may be prone to 'stalling' and this leads to a certain amount of frustration, so you need to plan a quiet evening – one which can really relax you and let the stress flow away. Be prepared for anything, be your adaptable self and you'll get through with a minimum of aggravation.

25 FRIDAY If your best plans go wrong it's important that you try to aim lower and prepare to build up more thoroughly and slowly towards getting what you want out of life. Remember, too, that if old methods no longer seem to be working, it may take time to replace them with something a little more imaginative; this means setting to one side current plans and projects. Be prepared to begin all over again.

26 SATURDAY Step back a little to review a situation. This has not been an easy time, but you can begin to see the light at the end of the proverbial tunnel. Emotionally, and maybe even domestically, you are transforming a rather difficult time into a garden of roses for the period ahead. It is slow going but the rewards will be great, so hang on.

27 SUNDAY Don't allow your personal life to lead you astray because there are so many other things that need your attention. Luckily, the stars today will help you to keep something in reserve, even though it may only just be enough. Loved ones will gladly take everything you have to offer right now, but don't count on getting a great deal back in return.

28 MONDAY Today is the day of the full Moon and it occurs in the fiery sign of Leo, the area of your chart devoted to career and work, so don't push other people beyond their limits otherwise you'll be creating a great deal of unpleasantness which won't reflect well on your character one little bit. Ideally, just stick to putting the finishing touches to jobs which have been left half done.

29 TUESDAY There could be some surprise developments, either in your emotional life or where socializing is concerned. Certainly you have a great deal of flair and originality about you when it comes to tackling any kind of problem, and it will be solved very quickly. There's a strong chance that you will be tempted to spend on extravagant pastimes and this needs conscious controlling.

30 WEDNESDAY There seems to be a great deal of scandal-mongering about at present but very little in the way of true facts, so refuse to accept what other people say unless you've a chance to have a look at the evidence for yourself. Cashwise, money must be handled with caution, not least because you are nowhere near as well off as you would like to think you are. In fact, an unexpected bill could very well catch you out.

31 THURSDAY The stars give you added inspiration which is sure to impress those on the working front, as well as your family. You're at your most ambitious, that's for sure, and because of this you will be reaching out into life in a more adventurous way and impressing everybody around. The evening looks set for romance so there's plenty to look forward to.

FEBRUARY

The Sun will be coasting along in Aquarius up until 18 February, and that's the area of your chart devoted to home and property affairs, which looks as if it's going to be extremely busy. Maybe you're entertaining friends at home and, if so, you're doing so with a great deal of ease, which other people will find charming.

From 19 February onwards, the Sun will be moving into Pisces, the area of your chart which hails the good times: great for those who are creative and those who simply want to have a good time. If you happen to be a parent, children will be a sheer delight at this time and you'll be very glad that you have them, even though at times you may have regretted it. Well, don't we all!

Mercury will be in retrograde movement until 7 February in the sign of Capricorn, the area of your chart devoted to home and family, so if you are buying property, you want to read the fine print very carefully, or better still get your solicitor to double check. Somebody could be out to pull the wool over your eyes and that would be a great pity. It might also be a good idea, if you have made social arrangements which involve people visiting your home, to keep in contact with them, as they may not be able to keep their promise and this will hurt you. You may be big and brave on the outside but you're as tender as any Pisces inside.

Venus will be coasting along in Aquarius for the first eleven days, and that's the area of your chart devoted to home and family, on which there seems to be a great deal of emphasis at this time. You'll be entertaining at home or there may simply be a great deal of harmony and love around. Those of you looking for somewhere to live shouldn't have any trouble whatsoever and will probably get property at a bargain price, and that can't be bad.

On 12 February, Venus will be moving on into Pisces, the area of your chart devoted to long distance travelling and higher education. If you're taking any kind of test or examination you will do well. Those of you worrying about people abroad can relax, you'll be hearing from them and the news will be good.

All month Mars will be in Aries, the area of your chart devoted to health, so you need to be careful. You will tire far more quickly than usual and there may be minor accidents, particularly where hot and sharp objects are concerned, so be extra careful when in the bathroom and kitchen – that's where most domestic accidents occur. A little bit of thought will take you a very long way indeed.

The pattern made by the stars this month suggests it is your personal and domestic life which will be dominating, rather than your professional life. It could be that work matters are ticking along nicely on their own, thank you very much, and they don't need a great deal of help from you.

1 FRIDAY You have added inspiration today which is sure to impress those on the working front, as well as your family. You're at your most ambitious, that's for sure, and because of this you will be reaching out into life in a more adventurous way and impressing everybody around. This evening looks set fair for romance so there's plenty to look forward to.

2 SATURDAY There's nothing you can do but be prepared to put your nose to the grindstone and attend to all the routine matters, which you find so boring. Never mind, you can't avoid them for ever, and besides, if you plan something special for the evening this will add impetus to your will-power, so see what you can do.

3 SUNDAY The stars suggest that you may be falling out with somebody, unless you're very careful. Conversely, it's an ideal time for bringing a set of circumstances to an end, if you feel that 'enough is enough'. The stars make this a useful day for putting the finishing touches to work, or for making plans for the future. Naturally, you're not going to rush into foolish actions, are you?

♏

4 MONDAY Today Mercury will be moving into Capricorn and that is the area of your chart devoted to the affairs of brothers and sisters, professional meetings and, to a degree, travelling. You can push ahead with alacrity in all of these areas, knowing that you're doing the right thing – it is always nice to get that extra bit of confidence, isn't it? If you have a Virgo or a Gemini in your life, they're going to make your time quite lively.

5 TUESDAY You've got a couple of days for pushing ahead with all self-interests, be they professional or personal. You've extra confidence, enthusiasm and imagination which is sure to impress everyone around. This is a particularly good time for the freelance worker, or the self-employed.

6 WEDNESDAY Today it's best to stick to the tried and tested rather than being too adventurous. Stress may take its toll and so, if you're feeling a little lacklustre, offload some of your work for the time being, until you're ready to zoom back into action once more, which won't be very long.

7 THURSDAY There's a certain amount of upheaval in at least one area of life. Luckily, you're an adaptable soul and are likely to view this as something of a challenge, which is the positive way to go. It might be a good idea to avoid mixing business with pleasure, because you'll find the company of colleagues boring, mainly due to the fact that all they wish to talk about is work, work, work.

8 FRIDAY This is good news day, because a couple of planets decide to resume direct movement and they are Mercury and Saturn. So where your life may have been unnecessarily

Monthly and Daily Guides: February

complicated up until now, from hereon in you can relax and push ahead, particularly if you want to travel or sign important documents.

9 SATURDAY This is an ideal time for sorting out official bureaucratic matters. Well, you have to at some time, otherwise they have a way of catching up with you, don't they? If you have any worries in connection with somebody else's financial stability, your worries will be put at rest in the near future. You need to relax this evening and let off a bit of steam.

10 SUNDAY Today is the day for being a bit more adventurous, so prepare to reach out into life and try the unknown; this applies to your emotional life as well as your professional life. If your work is at all related to foreign affairs there may be some exciting news which will certainly be livening up members of the staff as well as your good self too.

11 MONDAY Today, wherever you go, you'll be greeted by smiling faces and offers of help. Don't be too proud to ask for advice, as you'll be receiving some wise words. It's an excellent evening for romance, so make sure it doesn't go to waste; it may be a flirtatious time but that's the way you like it.

12 TUESDAY The new Moon today suggests that whatever plans you are currently involved with will eventually bring you some kind of reward or recognition. This aside, travel plans and social arrangements will bring a great deal of joy today. However, the stars do hint at secret rivals so make sure they don't get a chance to attack you on your own territory.

♏

13 WEDNESDAY The more daring you are, the more profitably your time will be spent. And, if you can persuade other people to go along with some crazy inspirations of yours, you'll be very glad they did. It's the unusual and eccentric approach to problems and ideas today which will certainly be paying off.

14 THURSDAY There's a good deal of movement on the working front. Lots of news will be making the rounds, some of which will need to be taken with a large grain of salt. You know how people exaggerate when they pass on news and that includes your good self, too.

15 FRIDAY Your mind is very much occupied with ambitions and your status. You'll be spending at least part of your time either phoning colleagues or making plans for the future. However, do ensure that you don't neglect your loved ones, because they're going to object in no uncertain fashion. On the other hand, if you're single, get on the phone to friends and plan an evening which is full of activity.

16 SATURDAY Others around seem to be running out of steam and it may be up to you to introduce some excitement as well as movement to the day. Luckily, you've got bags of energy. Where possible you should get in touch with nature if only for an hour. This will help to blow away the cobwebs, not only from yourself, but from your family and loved ones, too. You'll be ready then to give yourself over to the social whirl this evening.

17 SUNDAY A recent muddle connected with property, family or possibly a relative can be sorted out in record time.

This evening is an ideal one for entertaining at home, and you will be making a big impression. Romance can be pushed, if you have a mind to do so.

18 MONDAY Today the stars will help you to sense exactly what needs to be done, when and how. The only question which arises is, can you turn off your overactive brain and allow yourself to act on how you feel, instead of how you think. If you can do this, you'll be solving problems at the speed of light – it's up to you.

19 TUESDAY There's a strong indication from the stars that you should stay in the thick of all of the action, so don't think twice about staying in the limelight. In doing so you'll either be attracting the attentions of a potential lover, or making other people realize just how talented you really are.

20 WEDNESDAY You may suspect that someone is being anything but straight with you. If this is so, this would be the right time for a confrontation. However, make sure you remain calm, logical and fair-minded. It is a good time, too, for finding an outlet for one of your pet inspirations. You will find other people extremely receptive to you right now. This evening, give time to that special someone in your life.

21 THURSDAY There is a chance you may step on other people's toes at work today. It is also possible that the negative feelings of other people may rub off on you. This is because you are a chameleon and tend to blend into your surroundings. However, fight for your own individuality and remember that you are always master or mistress of your own fate.

♏

22 FRIDAY It is important to remember that no matter how hard life may have knocked you in the past, fear of living restricts you in a harmful way. Past events may have been hard, but now you have learned from them and you will be able to devote more time and attention to those who can fully appreciate your genuine enthusiasm, unconditional love and optimism. Basically, you have a good heart, despite what others may have taken from you and regardless of the emotional trials you have undergone.

23 SATURDAY Right now you will believe, quite correctly, that life is an experiment and that any worries and complications you encounter can be compared to a piece of machinery that is simply in need of some fuel. In life, your own and other people's trust is that fuel. By being too independent you frequently suffer from the feeling that everyone is against you. However, by working in harness with other people as you should be today, you will view the world through optimistic eyes.

24 SUNDAY Somebody else's behaviour, or words, will remove a lot of worry and heartache and restore your faith in a current project. You must, however, forget about your hurt pride or any cut or bruised ego. Whatever comes to light, remember that the past is history and only today and tomorrow count for anything at all.

25 MONDAY You may find old friends and acquaintances a little bit touchy. Don't exacerbate this situation by being critical or nosy. If they seem to want to spend time on their own, respect their privacy, because, after all, it is their right. As always, a time such as this will be a good one for making a few plans for the future.

♏

26 TUESDAY The planets are in an explosive mood and could make those closest to you a little bit rash and rather anxious – too much so to spend any kind of money. You may have to put your foot down, Scorpio. I know it's difficult for you to say 'no' but it's an absolute necessity during this particular day. Why not stand in front of the bathroom mirror and practise a couple of times before you go downstairs to greet whoever is waiting.

27 WEDNESDAY Today is the day of the full Moon and it occurs in the earthy sign of Virgo, the area of your chart devoted to team effort, club activities, friends and acquaintances, where there might be a certain amount of tension. If you don't feel like spending time with them, the best thing to do is to put your feet up at home, rather than go out and insult somebody and lose their friendship, which would be a great pity.

28 THURSDAY The stars suggest that you put your own needs first and ignore those who are accusing you of being selfish or self-centred – there's no such thing as a selfish Scorpio. You have wasted far too much time trying to be all things to all people; now you must follow your instincts, regardless of what anybody else tries to tell you are your obligations. Each and every day can be full of fun and laughter, providing you remember there is only one risk that isn't worth taking and that is the risk of doing nothing.

MARCH

The Sun will be coasting along in the water sign of Pisces up until 20 March, and that's the area of your chart devoted to matters related to abroad, foreign travel and education. In these areas you can be a little bit daring or, at the very least, confident, so push ahead.

After 20 March, the Sun will be moving into Aries, the area of your chart devoted to sheer hard slog, relationships with your workmates and your health. If you are feeling anything but 100 percent then it might be a good idea to visit your dentist or your doctor to get yourself back on track once more.

Mercury will be in Aquarius during the first eleven days and that's the area of your chart devoted to home and property, so if you are about to exchange contracts you've picked a good time for doing that. Failing this, entertaining at home will be a sheer joy; others will enjoy your hospitality and you'll be feeling good about yourself.

After 11 March, Mercury will be moving into Pisces, the area of your chart devoted to fun, games, children and creativity. Any, or all, of these can be pushed because you will be confident that you will do the right thing, at the right time, and you're perfectly correct.

Venus will be in Pisces up until 7 March, the area of your chart where you can let off steam, party all day and all night if you so desire, sort out children's needs and do exceptionally well on the creative front.

On 8 March, Venus will be moving into Aries and so work is emphasized, particularly if it happens to be artistic, or if you are in a partnership. Some of you may be attracted to a member of staff but if you already have a mate at home, for heaven's sake behave yourself, or else there will be trouble.

Mars makes its way through Taurus from the 2nd until the end of the month. That is, of course, your opposition, so you may be accident prone and you need to take care of hot and sharp objects, so be watchful in the kitchen or the bathroom. Furthermore, you may find that special person in your life becoming something of a 'sex maniac' – you will be surprised, but you will take delight in making the most of this, and who can possibly blame you.

The pattern made by the stars during this month seems to suggest that you will be mixing with people who are creative and go-getting. Some of them will be born under the signs of Pisces and Aries and if this should be the case, then stick with them, because this can do you a great deal of good.

1 FRIDAY Right now you seem to have your sights raised to an extremely high level, perhaps a little too high. If you trust your intuition, it will help to lead you to your chosen destination, and no matter how hard the journey, or difficult the climb, your arrival will please and impress those who care for you most.

2 SATURDAY There's a certain amount of excitement on the home front. Perhaps unexpected guests will arrive and you're delighted to see them. On the other hand, it may be that a member of the family is acting out of character and, if so, this is an ideal time for finding out why, as there may be something on their mind that they're reluctant to confide.

3 SUNDAY You seem to be in the mood for doing something 'different' – a new challenge, a new face – anything but boring routine will lure you away from home. And, if the phone remains horribly quiet, no doubt you'll make a few calls yourself and find some excuse to escape. Just make sure you don't offend a loved one. It might be a good idea to explain how you feel.

4 MONDAY The stars today suggest there is no reason why you should suffer in silence any longer. This is a time when you have the right to make the most of what is on offer. The skills and talents you were born with were meant to be used to make your life more varied and enjoyable, and over the next few days or so you'll get every chance to develop them to their fullest potential and you mustn't let it slip by.

5 TUESDAY Today, the last thing that's going to worry you is being bored. The phone rings constantly, both at work and at home, and there's plenty of chances for pleasure in the offing. All you have to do is to make up your mind exactly what you want to do and then plunge in at the deep end. Don't allow indecision to ruin your evening.

6 WEDNESDAY Just for once you decide that you are no longer going to keep a low profile and stay out of harm's way. If there seems to be any kind of trouble brewing then you will decide to meet it head on, and good for you. However, make sure that you don't go to extremes; strive as always to maintain some kind of balance because you need to be wise, to calm things down and not risk angering those closest to you, especially if they seem to be spoiling for a fight.

7 THURSDAY This is likely to be a day of minor changes and no end of opportunities in just about every area of life, but because you are at your most sensitive and secretive, you may find it hard to persuade partners, work colleagues, or loved ones to go along with your arrangements. If you don't have the confidence in yourself, how on earth can you expect others to have confidence in you?

Monthly and Daily Guides: March

8 FRIDAY It's important that you hold out for better conditions and don't let workmates, or even bosses, talk you out of what you're entitled to. The stars suggest that negotiations over career or cash matters still have a long way to go and that certain existing guarantees or promises are not as airtight as you believe. It's sad that each and every difficult journey in life tends to preface a new and more exciting chapter, but that doesn't mean you can permit others to walk all over you.

9 SATURDAY You seem to be under a great deal of emotional pressure lately and you're probably feeling run down and in need of rest, but don't count on getting it if you have certain partnership or domestic problems hanging in the air. Keep a watchful eye on money, too, because it would be the easiest thing in the world to let things slide simply because everything appears to be going well.

10 SUNDAY You can expect minor changes in connection with relationships, both at work and in your emotional life. However, there's no need for you to go into a complete flap: just take each new situation as it arises, adapt accordingly and leave yourself open to further movement. One thing is for sure, over the next couple of days or so, you can't take anything for granted.

11 MONDAY To a degree, the stars may dictate our circumstances but it's up to us to decide who will be our friends and who won't, and right now you really must ask yourself if you've chosen wisely. Even if the answer is 'no', there is still time to walk away from situations which have made your emotional life unsettled.

♏

12 TUESDAY Today Mercury will be moving into Pisces and that's the fun area of your chart. You could be drawn to intellectual pastimes, or maybe children are playing up quite considerably. Nevertheless, in your social life, lots of invitations are coming in for you to have fun, so try to balance your life as evenly as you can so that you can take advantage of everything.

13 WEDNESDAY Some of you will be signing lucrative contracts or at least hearing of them and must prepare to take advantage as soon as the situation seems right. If the opportunity to travel offers to swell your bank balance to a healthy level, don't even hesitate, accept because this could enrich you a great deal. It's a good time, too, for reviewing budgets.

14 THURSDAY Today is the day of the new Moon and it occurs in the watery sign of Pisces, the area devoted to children, creativity, sport and, above all else, flirting and fun. Make the most of this 24-hour period and be a little bit more daring; others will flock around you as you're looking good and feeling great.

15 FRIDAY Today the stars present you with a question about a certain close relationship. You are a sign who needs more support than you sometimes are prepared to admit, but you also need time, as well as space, to yourself for a moment. Intentions will fly out of the window at home and you need to watch that you're not rocking the boat too much.

16 SATURDAY The stars today encourage your love of colour, peace and harmony. They will also encourage your imagination and your intuition and, if you need these

Monthly and Daily Guides: March

particular qualities in your job, you'll certainly be doing well for yourself. Mind you, you are also advised to use that 'gut feeling' when in the company of new people this evening, just in case they are being anything but honest with you.

17 SUNDAY The stars could lower your energy levels and you're not entirely sure you know where you are aiming for at this time. When in doubt, do absolutely nothing, that's always good advice. Just give yourself enough space to recharge your batteries. Think about taking on some new health regime. Everyday companions are probably pushing you into saying more than is wise, but you mustn't allow yourself to be intimidated in this way, so take care.

18 MONDAY Those of you already committed to someone special may be seriously entertaining ideas of taking it a step further, and could become engaged or even married fairly soon. If so, you couldn't have picked a better time. For the unattached, there are so many opportunities to become involved with the opposite sex that you're positively spoiled for choice – have fun.

19 TUESDAY There could be one or two surprises in connection with friends or team mates. Somebody may be acting completely out of character and this rocks you on your heels, but rouses your curiosity. No doubt at some point you'll be attempting to get them on their own so you can find out what's really going on, well; it's only human to be a little cautious under such circumstances.

20 WEDNESDAY Work that involves detail and investigation will go well today and finances will take a turn for the better.

Family and friends are cooperative and helpful today, but by the evening you will need to be able to relax. Maybe you should curl up with that book you have been meaning to read for a while.

21 THURSDAY It looks as if you've been working very effectively and ambitiously recently, but it might be a good idea to take time to find some more peace and security, perhaps at home or with a loved one. You'll continue to make career ambitions your top priority for a while, but you will find that you need a solid emotional base as well. Be flirty, let your hair down a little more and have some fun, because you deserve it.

22 FRIDAY The stars will help you to make some wise and sensible decisions. Yes, unusually, you're not juggling with too many things at once but balancing them perfectly. If you need any kind of advice, go to an older and more experienced person, because they'll put you on the right track. This evening an older friend will be on the phone – perhaps he/she will want a favour.

23 SATURDAY Despite one or two background tensions and an inclination to let secrets slip, you seem to be in a mood to look further afield for fun and frolics in your life, but you can't quite make up your mind how to approach one set of discussions. Should you stand back and see the broad picture, or just get your head down? The answer will emerge without you having to look too hard for it. Be patient.

24 SUNDAY You can afford to paint on a broader canvas and think big thoughts, as well as act upon them. A project, or a person, you have long forgotten about suddenly emerges, much to your delight. Wherever you go at this time, you'll find a warm welcome and people who are ready to listen to your problems or your suggestions, so get out your courage, Scorpio, and be prepared to live life to the full.

25 MONDAY Your friends, contacts and acquaintances are going through a happy phase and their mood is definitely on the up and up, so if you are thinking of asking for any kind of favour or advice, this is most certainly the time for action. Socially you can have fun in any kind of sport.

26 TUESDAY There could be certain fluctuations where cash matters are concerned. It might be a good idea to hang on to your possessions, particularly when in crowds, because you may mislay something which may not be of financial value, but could hold pleasant memories which you wish to cling to. Be vigilant.

27 WEDNESDAY You must grab the opportunity to meet new people because you can never have too many friends or contacts. Besides, you need a great deal of stimulation, particularly this evening, so spending time on your own is not the way to go. Get out into life and grab your slice of the action.

28 THURSDAY Today is the day of the full Moon and it occurs in the airy sign of Libra. That, of course, is a rather secretive side to your chart and you must make sure you are not your own worst enemy. You could, for example, pass on secret information either of a professional or a personal nature, and this will come back to haunt you, so take care.

29 FRIDAY Today you could keep chopping and changing your mind to the point where other people are driven round the bend and back again. The best thing to do is to stick to minor decisions and refuse to discuss anything major for the time being, because you'll only cause a great deal of bad feeling and that simply won't do. Don't be surprised, either, if a social arrangement this evening is subject to last minute changes or adjustments; you need to be flexible.

30 SATURDAY It seems you're trying to do too much because you're making sure that you are doing everything possible to please others and trying to keep fit at the same time, which is quite an undertaking. If you're not careful your energy will take a nose-dive later on in the day. So allow yourself to retreat into your own company at least for an hour or so in order to wind down.

31 SUNDAY Luckily the stars are helping you to look ahead with confidence and you can feel the urge to kick up your heels, enjoy yourself and spend just a little more than is really wise. Maybe you do need to hit the brake when thinking about indulging yourself, but much depends on your financial state.

APRIL

The Sun will be drifting along in the fiery sign of Aries up until 19 April and that's the area of your chart devoted to sheer hard slog, so there's no point in thinking you're going to get away with anything, Scorpio – roll up your sleeves, pitch in and others will appreciate all of your efforts.

On 20 April, the Sun will be moving into Taurus and that,

Monthly and Daily Guides: April

of course, is your opposite number, so a great deal of your concentration, time and effort will be going out into your close relationships. Don't think you'll be wasting your time, as others are going to appreciate everything you put out. Should you be fancy free, then you've got an ideal time for socializing as much as possible because there's somebody out there for you somewhere, Scorpio; all you've got to do is find them – see what you can do.

Mercury will be in Aries until 12 April, so it's still important that you pamper yourself. You're going to run out of energy more than is usually the case, so take it easy. There will be opportunities for travelling too, but unless you're feeling 100 percent fit it might be a good idea to turn it down for the time being; the chance to do so will arise some time in the future, never fear.

Venus enters your opposite sign of Taurus on 1 April, where it stays until the 25th, so other people are going to be kind, gentle, sociable and, above all else, romantic. See if you can slot in with these moods as they occur so that you can increase compatibility and perhaps get to know other people a little bit better.

After 25 April, Venus will be moving on into Gemini, throwing a rosy glow over financial affairs, both yours and other people's, particularly on the working front. If you need a time to chat to your bank manager do so as soon as possible because he/she will be in a good mood.

Mars will remain in Taurus during the first thirteen days, which will make those closest to you rather argumentative, quarrelsome and accident prone. See what you can do to protect them if you think they're being a little bit too rash. Naturally they will object to any interference but if you express your words with charm and love how can you possibly fail to make your point. On 14 April Mars will move into Taurus and this is not a time to take any liberties with those in authority, whether it is your boss or your bank manager. If you take this advice you will avoid a lot of aggravation in the long run.

The pattern made by the stars suggests that other people have a great deal of influence on you over this month. There's no point in kicking against this and rebelling; the best thing you can do is to listen to all the advice that you are getting and then, at a later date, sit down and sift out which you think is valid and which should be ignored. Naturally, as a Scorpio, you do not like being advised, you always think you know best, but look back on your past history, Scorpio, is this true? Somehow I doubt it. Maybe it's time for a re-think then.

1 MONDAY Home matters seem happier, calmer and more together than they have been for a long while, so don't worry if a close friend wants a longer rein today. Make sure you're keeping an eye on any long-term career aims too, because this is a time for thinking about sowing a few seeds. They may not seem to flourish for a while, but they should get off to a settled start, at least, and that's something.

2 TUESDAY This is a day which could be full of hustle and bustle. Yes, it's a busy patch at the moment and you have many great ideas floating around your head, you have visits to make, phone calls to answer and letters to write. Just take some time to step back and clear the decks, even if it's only a few minutes, otherwise you'll get yourself into one hell of a mess. Life with those closest to you seems to be a bit touchy, so it's important that you remember to be your usual tactful, charming self.

3 WEDNESDAY Certainly, where interviews, negotiations, communications and documents are concerned, you need a great deal of double checking to avoid muddle and confusion which will run rife if you're careless. Not a good time for presenting new ideas to other people because right now they are unlikely to be receptive.

4 THURSDAY You temporarily take on a different persona, becoming more down to earth, practical and even downright stubborn. Still, at least this will stop others taking you for granted quite so much and many people who thought they knew you well will have to rethink quite seriously. It's quite nice to be something of a devil for a change, isn't it?

5 FRIDAY This day could be full of muddle, confusion and mystery unless you get yourself seriously organized and double check all of your arrangements. Leave nothing to chance, because if something can go wrong, it most certainly will. Make sure, too, that you don't allow your emotions to take flight; you could imagine yourself to be in love with somebody who is completely unsuitable.

6 SATURDAY Your heart is most likely going to be ruling your head today, certainly where cash matters are concerned, and this is a bit worrying. Even so, with any luck, the outcome could be sparkling and in many ways great fun, but hardly comforting to your bank manager who may be chewing his fingernails down to his elbow – not that you'll be worrying about that.

7 SUNDAY One thing is quite clear about your future progress – fitting in with everybody else's plans is going to be important. You really can't afford to strike out totally independently or even call the shots. Luckily, though, you're an adaptable sort who can generally find the best solution to difficult problems.

8 MONDAY There could be a good deal of mystery, muddle and confusion around you. Don't take the words or promises of other people too seriously and even adopt a fairly cynical attitude towards your own reactions. The planets have a way of throwing a cloud of secrecy and mystery over matters so that we can no longer see them for what they are. The best thing you can do is to plan a routine.

9 TUESDAY Today is the time for making your own arrangements, in your own sweet time, and refuse to be affected by the whims and so-called inspirations of other people. It wouldn't be a good idea to make it too much of a late night either because, quite frankly Scorpio, this is a time when you need some rest.

10 WEDNESDAY If you have a flatmate, it's likely you might be seriously worried about whether they can meet their end of the expenses. If this should be the case then the sensible thing to do is to sit them down at some point over the next couple of days and find out what is really going on, because only then will you be in the know and able to make plans for the future.

11 THURSDAY This is certainly not a time for hoping for a raise or expecting a tempting offer to materialize; instead, use this period for putting the finishing touches to the many jobs you've left unfinished and use this evening for allowing stress to melt away. Certainly avoid the company of those who irritate because you may uncharacteristically tell them what you think of them.

12 FRIDAY This is the day of the new Moon and it occurs in the fiery sign of Aries, the area of your chart devoted to health, which should be flourishing, and work, which seems to be going in a positive direction. As always with new Moons we can all be a little more daring and that includes you – so if there's someone special you quite fancy, then this evening might be a good time to give them a call.

13 SATURDAY Other people's faults and failings appear to be causing you a great deal of unnecessary irritation. There is, though, sufficient strength in your personal armoury to stand up to any kind of emotional onslaught. The stars today are urging you to state your case and make your point while you still have the chance to get a word in edgeways. Boring obligations may distract you from what really matters, but think of them as payments into the deposit account of life.

14 SUNDAY Today Mars will be moving into Gemini and that's the area of your chart devoted to people you are financially dependent upon. You may find bosses and supervisors a little tense and irritable, so turn on the charm but don't overdo it otherwise they'll see right through you.

15 MONDAY A close companion or workmate seems to be on edge and you are probably wondering how to rescue, reconcile and resolve the situation. However, the stars seem to suggest that you will find it easier to pour oil on troubled waters in the very near future and may have to be patient in the meantime. New ideas, choices or opportunities are all in the air, but you need a clear head and a willing heart to take advantage of them.

16 TUESDAY Today you will start to consider new slants on old problems and situations, because it is the new and untried which is likely to be successful on this particular day. So throw your old routine or ingrained habits out of the window as soon as possible.

17 WEDNESDAY You know, Scorpio, there's little point in robbing from Peter to pay Paul. Your cash situation may be far from ideal just now, but it could be considerably worse, that's one consolation. In the not too distant future you'll have a far better chance of agreeing realistic long-term settlements and arrangements. Remember there is an enormous gap between advice and help.

18 THURSDAY You need to be especially careful when in the company of friends, contacts and acquaintances because, quite unintentionally, it'll be all too easy for you to offend them in some way. Better still, be as independent as you can, mind your own business and wait for the mood to pass. Naturally, you can't avoid the entire human race, but if you can turn on that charm of yours then maybe this will help to calm troubled waters.

19 FRIDAY This is certainly a time when it would be a good idea to dip your toes in the water of opportunity but, unless you are ready to get completely wet, you will never make it to the opposite shore. You are, however, advised to dive in before someone else beats you to it. Certainly the stars will help to provide for your worldly needs.

Monthly and Daily Guides: April

20 SATURDAY It certainly seems that others are calling all the shots and you really must avoid being in the line of fire. The stars right now are trying to help you to revise certain priorities to take account of your personal needs, demands and desires. It's all very well being able to smile in the face of adversity but you must also be able to cry when the occasion demands it.

21 SUNDAY The Sun has now moved into Taurus and that's the area of your chart devoted to partnership. You will become much more giving than is usually the case and other people are going to be impressed. If someone close to you is in trouble you will be the one who will be riding to the rescue and you'll be gleaning the praise at a later date.

22 MONDAY The stars should lift your spirits and encourage you to grab all social and romantic opportunities. There may be some unexpected ups and downs where money is concerned, but you sense that things are on the up and so are unlikely to be getting yourself too upset.

23 TUESDAY Someone may ask your name and temporarily your mind goes blank. We've all experienced this from time to time and, of course, it makes us feel foolish. Never mind, luckily, other people seem to be in a forgiving mood, but even so it won't be a good idea to take anything for granted, so double check where possible.

24 WEDNESDAY As long as you're honest with those in positions of power and influence, you have nothing to fear. It's only the Scorpio who tries to be a little bit too clever who could come severely unstuck today. As always, you must strive to be as scrupulous as possible: if a Scorpio can't do this then I don't know who else can. It might be a good idea to keep out of the limelight.

25 THURSDAY Today's stars suggest that you are now in a position to run rings around those who have doubted your talents in the past. That doesn't mean, however, that you should demand more than you deserve – don't be greedy. The stars are allowing you to air your ambitions and prove your authority, but there are other considerations which are part of the final puzzle.

26 FRIDAY It's a good time for travelling or contacting people abroad, and you have no need to fear signing any kind of contract, always assuming, of course, that you have it checked first. Yes, you have the green light from the stars to push ahead in any area your little heart desires.

27 SATURDAY Today is the day of the full Moon and it occurs in the watery sign of Scorpio. That, of course, is your sign, so if you are feeling under the weather, generally disillusioned, or just plain grumpy, don't take anything too seriously. Fortunately, full Moons soon wear off and by late tomorrow you'll be back to your normal self.

28 SUNDAY Today you still have to make up your changeable mind about where you want to end up and with whom. Being adventurous, creative and enterprising isn't enough when there is so much at stake, as there is right now. Today, you must gather your thoughts before stating your case. Wisdom means talking a little bit less, but saying a great deal more.

♏

29 MONDAY Many of you may decide that it's time to do some studying in order to increase your chance of success for the future. If you decide to do this, at a later date you'll realize it was perhaps the most important move you have made for years. Romantically, it's interesting accents and exotic people who are likely to appeal.

30 TUESDAY There's no point in expecting other people to grant favours on this particular day, as they're not in the mood. Soldier on alone for the time being; it won't do you any harm, and you may even decide that being independent is something you should cultivate in the future and, in actual fact, you are quite right, because it never pays to be too dependent.

MAY

The Sun will be coasting along in your opposite number of Taurus up until 20 May. That's the area of your chart devoted to partnerships and other people and so, Scorpio, there's no point in you constantly expecting to have your own way. Especially where loved ones are concerned, you must go out of your way to find out exactly what it is that they want from you, because only in that way will you know how to behave. The fate of your relationships is in your hands this month, so do make sure that you act wisely.

After 20 May, the Sun will be moving into Gemini, the area of your chart devoted to people you are financially dependent upon, such as your boss or maybe your partner. Your bank manager may have several things to say, too, particularly if you have an overdraft and, if so, you will need to have a meeting with him/her and sort things out before matters get out of control.

♏

Mercury will also be coasting along in Gemini all month, which is borne out by the amount of mail that you receive. Hopefully it's all good news but there are bound to be a few disconcerting bills from time to time. Hopefully, you've been your usual sensible self and put the money away so that you can pay them without any difficulty at all.

Venus will be in Gemini until 20 May and, once again, that's the area of your chart devoted to people you are financially dependent upon and, to a degree, your emotional life. If you are a true Scorpio, you hate to be in debt and if this should be the case this month you're going to be taking out your frustration on your loved ones. In a word – don't – they will not appreciate it and it could even lead to the end of a relationship, which would be a great pity. From the 21st, Venus will be coasting along in Cancer. If you are single this is a great time for romance, particularly with those from foreign lands. Even if you are at home, you are sure to be hearing from those abroad.

Believe it or not, Mars is also in the sign of Gemini until 27 May, encouraging rash spending, arguments over money and tension in this area. Fortunately, you've bought this little book and if you listen to the advice that you are given, with any luck at least you will be able to minimize problems; if not obliterate them completely.

The pattern made by the stars puts the emphasis on your home, emotional and sexual life, rather than on the need to keep climbing the ladder of success. This makes a pleasant change for those who love you and they will take full advantage and probably give you as much pampering as you can take which, let's face it, is quite considerable. All in all there's a lot to look forward to, providing you avoid the pitfalls.

♏

Monthly and Daily Guides: May

1 WEDNESDAY You could end today all the poorer if you're not careful. It would be a good idea to avoid the more expensive shops, because even within the space of ten minutes you can do considerable damage to your bank account. Leave the plastic at home, too, and make sure those special little valuables of yours are tucked away in a safe place. Double check change.

2 THURSDAY There's an emphasis on foreign affairs, travel and further education, and so many of you will decide it's time to take on some fresh study in order to increase your chances of success for the future. In times to come, you will look back and realize what an important decision this was.

3 FRIDAY Don't take anything for granted but do a great deal of double checking because in this way you'll avoid unnecessary stress. The stars signify that friends and acquaintances are in a changeable mood so if you have any arrangements with them it might be a good idea to get on the phone and check, just in case they've forgotten or changed their minds.

4 SATURDAY You seem to have reached some kind of crossroads in a cash or property matter and now there are major decisions which really have to be made. Today's aspects will force you to raise your voice as well as your expectations. You may feel you are being taken in by what is going on around you, but it is more of an excuse than a reality. Give yourself time to take stock before you leap into action.

5 SUNDAY The stars prompt you to rekindle family closeness and perhaps be drawn to the intimacy of your own home. It's likely that you'll find personal security through meeting a challenge in the future, and this is the time when you can draw comfort from what has been established in the past. Chewing things over with those closest to you will prove to be fruitful.

6 MONDAY The stars today encourage you to be in an unusually playful frame of mind to consider choices you would never have entertained in the past. However, one deciding factor in whether or not you actually go the whole hog, depends on the support you can generate from someone close to you. By the end of this day you will have been able to make up your mind whether or not to tie the knot on a project, venture or commitment.

7 TUESDAY Go after whatever or whoever you want, and don't be afraid to ask a few favours either. They will most certainly be granted. It's a good day for party-going, sports and, if you are a parent, for opening up the lines of communication between yourself and your offspring. All in all a lively day.

8 WEDNESDAY It may be true that the road of life has recently been bumpy, but it hasn't been without its more tantalizing opportunities. Right now, the stars seem to create an atmosphere which blows hot one moment and cold the next, but the all-important thing at this moment in time is that they promise a fresh start in connection with your earnings and what you owe. Therefore, it's important that you are as confrontational as possible where cash matters are concerned.

9 THURSDAY Your friends and contacts are in an intuitive, inspired and creative frame of mind. Now, if you think you could do with a touch of these qualities, don't be afraid to ask

Monthly and Daily Guides: May

them because they'll be only too willing to help you out in any way they can. This evening you want to spend time with gentle but colourful people, as anyone who is loud or crude will get on your nerves.

10 FRIDAY Any travelling, be it for personal or professional reasons, will be thoroughly enjoyable, and new people who enter your life will become fast friends, not only lending a helping hand but giving you some excellent advice, if only you can bring yourself to follow it. Get together your courage, Scorpio, because the braver and more adventurous you are, the better the next couple of weeks will be.

11 SATURDAY Do take extra care when travelling, because you may miss connections, be involved in snare-ups, or have difficulty with your mode of transport. If there was ever a day when you were going to run out of petrol in the most inconvenient spot in the world, this is likely to be it, so you have been warned.

12 SUNDAY Today is the day of the new Moon and it occurs in your opposite sign of Taurus, so it's likely that other people will be in an adventurous, giving and devil-may-care mood. Whatever you do, don't discourage them, let them let off a bit of steam – after all, they certainly need it and, probably, so do you.

13 MONDAY This is a time when you simply must take stock of your personal and cash commitments. Even though you were born under a fairly canny sign of the zodiac, still you can't continue to let people dictate the terms of your lifestyle. Some people may not be deliberately trying to take you for a ride but, nevertheless, they are becoming accustomed to seeing you as a liability and so you must steer clear of their whims and their demands.

14 TUESDAY Communications could become unnecessarily complicated and you need to follow instructions to the letter and even ask that they be repeated if necessary. Furthermore, read letters through at least twice and if you don't understand something a friend is trying to tell you on the phone, don't hesitate to ask them to repeat it. Too often you worry about what other people think, but it is better to be safe than sorry, you must admit.

15 WEDNESDAY Today Mercury decides to go into retrograde movement and, because of this, if you have a Gemini or Virgo in your life they could become rather tiresome over the next few weeks. Furthermore, it is not a time for unnecessary travelling or for signing on the dotted line. If you do, you're going to regret it, I can assure you.

16 THURSDAY You could be in an extravagant mood, or there's a possibility that you may lose a possession whilst on the move. The best thing to do is to leave your credit cards at home and those precious little treasures of yours in a safe place, but not about your person. Other people's ideas for having fun may be a little too pricey for you at this time.

17 FRIDAY Important talks today will give you a clearer idea of the merits of pushing ahead with an idea which promises to present you with a giant leap up the ladder of success. Unfortunately, you're inclined to be a little irritable with those who advise caution or restraint, but as long as you can

Monthly and Daily Guides: May

manage to stay on the middle path, which you are usually pretty good at, no harm will come to you.

18 SATURDAY The planets are advising you to be more prepared to take a risk, to be adventurous and, above all else, not to shrink from asking advice from other people. You may also experience being in the right place at the right time when Dame Fortune sails past and, if so, you must be quick to recognize the fact and milk it for all it's worth.

19 SUNDAY You might start the day off a little bit slowly, perhaps due to yesterday's activities, but as the hours pass you gather momentum, imagination and creativity. There's something sparkling and irresistible about you right now, so if you need any kind of favour, be it in your professional or personal life, you mustn't hesitate to push forward, because others are most likely to be ready to help you in any way they can.

20 MONDAY Today the stars are romantic and a bit sparkly. The long-drawn-out presence of some of the planets has concentrated your mind on responsibilities and, at times, significantly reduced your love of life. However, right now there isn't a planet anywhere that can restrain you. You're determined to put your heart and soul into everything and everyone you are involved with. You'll be gleaning a great deal of admiration and others will be seeing you in a much more positive light.

21 TUESDAY Today Venus will be moving into Cancer, the area of your chart devoted to long distance travelling, insurance matters and foreign affairs in general. Furthermore, you could become somewhat over-idealistic where the behaviour of other people is concerned, but unless you're perfect yourself, Scorpio, you've no right to expect such behaviour from others at all.

22 WEDNESDAY The Sun is now in the airy sign of Gemini and that's the area of your chart devoted to health, so if you're feeling under the weather it might be a good idea to visit your doctor or dentist. If not, don't take any chances when driving or crossing the road, if anyone's going to get knocked down it could be you – you have been warned, so please take the advice.

23 THURSDAY Over the past few days or so there's been an increasing amount of action in partnership matters or perhaps business ventures. All the signposts in life suggest you stand to gain much more from joining forces rather than going out on a limb on your own. Don't for one moment imagine, however, that those who want to support you will stop you investigating the inner aspects of your plans or financial arrangements.

24 FRIDAY You may be only too aware of the need to take an enormous jump into the unknown, but you still seem to have difficulties making a final break. This is an excellent day for giving yourself a good talking to, because you must start to move with all speed as soon as possible. Freedom means the right to be different, the right to live your life, and to do so using your own principles and rules.

25 SATURDAY There's a rosy glow over professional matters over the next couple of days. Those of you who are either

Monthly and Daily Guides: May

hoping to land a job, or perhaps promotion, will hear some news which will make you realize that your professional dreams are about to come true. This will be a particularly lucky few days for you, Scorpio, especially if you're involved in professional partnerships or creative work, because imagination is firing on all cylinders.

26 SUNDAY Today is the day of the full Moon and it occurs in the fiery sign of Sagittarius, the area of your chart devoted to finances, so you've got to be careful during this period, otherwise you'll spend recklessly and be paying for it for many moons to come – take care.

27 MONDAY You are likely to be considering various possibilities and your friends and acquaintances will be quick to chip in with their suggestions. Mind you, this could only create greater confusion but it's up to you to listen to that small voice within rather than allowing yourself to be pulled in various directions by other people.

28 TUESDAY Those closest to you are at their most energetic, passionate and sexy and you'll have a hard time keeping up with them; don't allow one of those lazy moods of yours to take over, otherwise you'll find yourself seriously missing out. Offers of help are likely to come in and because you are not in a proud mood, you'll be willing to grab at anything that even hints at a possible opportunity for you.

29 WEDNESDAY There may be a forgotten bill that suddenly turns up, or a small emergency which means you have to dig deeper into your pockets. On no account make the situation worse by giving in to a bout of extravagance, because if you do, by the time the evening comes, you'll find yourself all the poorer.

30 THURSDAY The stars will be encouraging a positive mood where family and property matters are concerned. If somebody at home is being uncooperative, or even mysterious, now is the time to sit them down and find out exactly what's going on. Those of you looking for a new home should step up your efforts on this day because you could find exactly what you're looking for.

31 FRIDAY Money seems to be going to waste, Scorpio. Now this simply won't do, because unless you've just won the lottery, this is the time for economizing in order to increase your sense of security for the near future. You may also find that other people keep changing their minds over money; the best thing you can do is to detach yourself from them and stay as independent as you possibly can.

JUNE

The Sun will be drifting along in the airy sign of Gemini up until 21 June, and that's the area of your chart devoted to sheer hard slog, which must be tackled, and health, which should not be undermined in any way, shape or form. In fact, if you feel a little shaky or overtired make sure that you get in several early nights, as that will improve this matter no end.

On 22 June, the Sun will be moving into Cancer, a water sign like your good self, and this part of your chart is devoted to foreign affairs and legal affairs, so adventure on all sides seems to be highlighted. Reach out into life far more than you usually do because you won't regret it if you do.

Monthly and Daily Guides: June

Mercury will be in Gemini all month, and there's a certain amount of movement with people you are financially dependent upon. Where your work is concerned it may be necessary for you to take a short trip and, if so, volunteer to do it, as this could be extremely beneficial.

Venus will be in Cancer early in the month, again placing the emphasis on foreign affairs and also on your ideals, which seem to be incredibly high at this time. You'll need to adopt a practical approach to them in order to make sure that you're on the right path, as there's a distinct possibility that you may not.

After 14 June, Venus moves into Leo, throwing a rosy glow over your ambitions and work in general, particularly if it happens to be artistic or if you're in a partnership. You can afford to be a little bit cheeky at this time and let other people know exactly what you're thinking and what you're feeling and what your brilliant ideas are really all about. If you can do that, you can make this month quite a startling one.

Mars will be in the watery sign of Cancer all June. If you are studying for an exam or test, take things slowly and carefully. To rush things would be a disaster as well as causing bad feelings amongst those close to you.

The pattern made by the stars seems to suggest that people born under the sign of Leo and Cancer will be all important to your progress during this period. It's difficult for a Scorpio ever to ask for help, even from close relatives, never mind strangers, but just review all opportunities that come your way, think about them for a couple of days and if they seem to be viable to you then say, 'yes', in a loud voice and push ahead because you're not going to be sorry.

1 SATURDAY This is likely to be a lively day. People you haven't heard from for simply ages get in touch; it may even take you a few minutes to realize who you're actually speaking to – yes, it's been that long. Still, it's always nice to have a chance to catch up with all the gossip. And rekindling old bonds could in some way enrich you, if not financially then emotionally. Be ready to say yes to all chances that crop up from an unexpected quarter.

2 SUNDAY You'll be drawn to people not only because of the way they look, but unusually, you're looking deeper into their souls and into their minds and in doing so you'll find somebody who is really worthwhile. Mind you, if you already happen to have a partner, you'll need to keep those emotions under tight control, otherwise there could be an almighty explosion at a later date. On the other hand, if your existing relationship is well past its sell-by date, you may consider launching into life with somebody new.

3 MONDAY Today Uranus goes into retrograde movement, and that is the area of your chart devoted to home, so where property matters and home entertaining are concerned, things will get into a real muddle if you allow them to. Maybe it would be a good idea to re-think and make arrangements for later on in the month; that would be the wisest thing to do anyway. Should you have an Aquarian close to you they will also be getting in a muddle, perhaps even more than you.

4 TUESDAY Conflicting news seems to be turning your world inside out and it might be difficult to know whether or not to continue your fight for a fair settlement. Accept the fact that what's gone is gone, and that your energies must now be channelled into something original and tried. You'll have plenty of time to sit down and make some plans for the future, so your time will not be wasted.

5 WEDNESDAY It's difficult for you to work out how a calculated gamble is likely to develop over the next couple of days or so. Mind you, you don't have to sit it out alone, because there are several sympathetic and supportive people within your circle who are ready to 'be there' for you. All you need to do to get them on your side and to obtain their help is to simply ask.

6 THURSDAY Everybody you meet today is likely to be hypersensitive, creative or a little bit absent-minded. Mind you, this could come as something of a relief because it's always nice to know that other people can be equally as disorganized on occasions, isn't it? This aside, though, today could be a red letter day for romance and certainly you're going to be approached by admirers.

7 FRIDAY A chance for progress is certainly not going to escape your notice now, even the smallest sparkle of an idea can be developed until at least one of your ambitions is achieved. The only danger is the possibility that in channelling your vitality in too many directions, you could spread yourself over too wide an area and miss out.

8 SATURDAY Today Mercury finally decides to see sense and resumes direct movement, so from hereon in you need not fear signing documents, going on trips, or meeting new people. Clearly a period is starting when you can be a little bit more adventurous – see that you are.

♏

9 SUNDAY Setting up a new phase of your life is exciting but usually makes you feel edgy. However, you are quite rightfully full of bounce and confidence. You have overcome several problems recently and feel much more in control of both team situations and long-term plans. The stars encourage you to go onwards and upwards all the way. You're beginning to feel you can handle almost anything, and anyone.

10 MONDAY Today is the day of the new Moon and it occurs in the airy sign of Gemini, the area of your chart devoted to people you are financially dependent upon. So your boss, your supervisor or even your mate at home will have some ideas for change and that's not a word that you like too much now, is it Scorpio? However, give everybody a listen and then think about it for a couple of days before you turn them down.

11 TUESDAY Nobody, least of all me, is going to argue with the fact that you have had certain difficulties recently. However, in the days to come you will be thankful that you were put to the test and were able to establish yourself both on a professional level and personally too. Very soon, the present turbulence will be blown away and forgotten.

12 WEDNESDAY The stars today are certainly activating your imagination, but regrettably in a negative way. The thing to do is to keep yourself as busy as possible – think thoughts of sunshine rather than doom and gloom, or you may attract that which you most fear.

Monthly and Daily Guides: June

13 THURSDAY Right now you may feel that life seems to have forced you into becoming a prisoner of your own responsibility. Because of the planetary set-up today, you will see things in a new perspective very soon. What you must try to bear in mind is that you are free to move wherever and whenever you want to, so there's no point in trying to find excuses for marking time because, basically, there aren't any and other people are only too aware of the fact.

14 FRIDAY The stars could bring news, perhaps from abroad, of an intriguing offer, and this is certainly stimulating your interest. Even so, you appear unable to make up your mind, possibly due to the fact that you believe the terms and consequences are yet to be clarified. Whatever you do, don't let minor details endanger important opportunities.

15 SATURDAY Today Venus will be moving into Leo, the area of your chart devoted to your career, so there's a rosy glow over all professional matters and your relationship with workmates is on the up and up. Some of you may even form a love affair with somebody you meet whilst going about your duties. That's all well and good if you happen to be single, but if not you are letting yourself in for a hell of a lot of trouble.

16 SUNDAY You're a good-natured, sweet tempered person for the most part but right now the stars may be encouraging you to speak your mind in no uncertain fashion, but it's important that you say no more than is absolutely necessary. Exchange of opinions will do much to clear the air, but, bear in mind you are privy to certain information which was meant for nobody's ears but your own. Discretion should be your watch-word.

♏

17 MONDAY Where finances are concerned you are likely to have a rather inflated view about how much you have tucked away in the bank. Before you go out into the big wide world waving your plastic, it might be a good idea to ring the bank and check on the amount you have available because, quite frankly, you can't afford to make financial mistakes at this time and, if you do, you'll be paying for it for some while.

18 TUESDAY No matter how much you cajole, or try to bring your influence to bear on professional proceedings, little progress has been made for the time being. The truth of the matter is that others are reluctant to change their attitudes until they have the willingness to change them for themselves. No amount of bullying or persuasion will have any effect.

19 WEDNESDAY A whole series of professional hurdles will stay in place just as long as you continue to refuse to change your attitude towards them. Right now all kinds of chances and opportunities will be popping up and whatever else you do, you must avoid hiding behind old-fashioned thinking or ideas. Open up your mind to fresh horizons and be ready to take up the challenge.

20 THURSDAY Today the stars suggest that it is time to open your mind and your emotions to something different and exciting, perhaps you've been stuck in a rut for far too long. Other people are perfectly willing to educate you when it comes to new ways of tackling work. However, only you can throw off the chains of your own daily existence and let yourself travel further in unchartered waters.

♏

Monthly and Daily Guides: June

21 FRIDAY Because you have been urged to try the impossible, you have probably found yourself repeating patterns or routines which have left you feeling deserted and isolated, and now the stars will help you to concentrate on those responsibilities which bring you the greatest fulfilment. You're not exactly sure what these are, but it might be a good idea to take some time out in order to draw up a list of priorities then work your way through them.

22 SATURDAY Today the Sun will be moving into the water sign of Cancer, the area of your chart devoted to your career, and you are going to be very 'one pointed'. When a Scorpio really puts her or his nose to the grindstone and is determined to achieve, heaven help anybody that gets in the way. However, try to be a little considerate of other people's feelings as you go along, otherwise they'll try and get you at a later date and that would be a pity.

23 SUNDAY Few things are more annoying than people who are determined to argue. Although conflicts may be inevitable, the revelations should be worth the trouble. Equally, however unsettling, changes in your daily routine or working life are overdue. Let decisions wait for a couple of days and then you'll need only make them once.

24 MONDAY Whatever you say, someone is going to be unhappy, but don't let that make you think that something has gone wrong. The conflicts indicated by difficult aspects enable you to settle issues – some minor, others important – and then forget them. Having made the decisions, it will boost your confidence and you can then consider more far-reaching changes.

♏

25 TUESDAY It may seem to you that in disputing certain issues other people are getting at you – a feeling that the stars accentuate today. Behind this, however, are important matters and studying these is illuminating and equips you for important opportunities that you can expect over the next couple of days.

26 WEDNESDAY If your instincts tell you that others' commitments are only half-hearted or that circumstances could force them to alter arrangements, you may be right. The stars indicate the end of one cycle and the beginning of another, so be prepared to face up to dramatic developments.

27 THURSDAY It's difficult to imagine you getting through the day without receiving either an excellent financial offer, or the welcome arrival of a cheque that is well overdue. Mind you, your first reaction may be to hit the shops in a big way, but this isn't a clever thing to do, Scorpio. Certainly, you can afford to treat yourself modestly, but if you've any common sense at all, you'll put the majority of your loot away for the proverbial rainy day when it's sure to pour down.

28 FRIDAY Regardless of whether your problems are connected with romantic affairs or financial matters, certain people will regret having taken you for a fool. A period of disillusionment and a certain amount of hurt is coming to an end, but you must be prepared to give short shrift to anyone who is making an effort to stop you from planning the future.

29 SATURDAY Few can resist your abundant charm at this time and so you are provided with a day for asking favours and even taking a few small liberties. An unusual invitation is also likely to be heading in your direction and the lure of romance and the bright lights will be difficult for you to resist, so why bother.

30 SUNDAY There could be a certain amount of tension and because of this you need to spend your time in pleasant surroundings with people who have a calming effect on you. Don't allow rivals and competitors to apply pinpricks to your ego because you will easily be deflated.

JULY

The Sun will be coasting along in the water sign of Cancer up until 22 July, and that's the area of your chart devoted to friends, contacts and associates, all of whom seem to be in a good mood. So if you need any kind of favour you only need to ask, but do so applying that little word 'please', of course.

On 23 July, the Sun will be moving into Leo so, from now on, while this state of affairs exists, you will become very single-minded, at your most ambitious, treading on other people's toes, pinching their ideas and generally determined to reach the top of the totem pole where you believe you belong.

Mercury will be sailing through Gemini for the first five days of July, the area which represents legal matters and people you are financially dependent upon, so any problems in connection with these sides to life should be tackled immediately because this is a fine time for doing just that. Any chance to travel for the sake of your job should be snapped up; it will be all-important to you. On the 6th, Mercury will float into Cancer and this is a good time for taking tests and exams. Mentally you are now razor sharp so no one can get one over on you – and they had better not try!

Venus will be in the fiery sign of Leo for the first ten days of July, making this a very sociable time. If you get out to bars or clubs you are bound to make some new friends. On a more serious note, this is also a good moment for sorting out any legal matters. On 11 July Venus coasts into Virgo and now team effort becomes the key. New friends could prove useful to you and they might also introduce you to new pastimes and activities.

Mars will be coasting along in Cancer during the first 13 days, generating in you a certain amount of impulse which basically needs to be controlled, otherwise you'll get yourself in trouble one way or the other.

From 14 July onwards, Mars will be coasting along in Leo, again emphasizing tremendous hard work but, of course, you are as strong as an ox and very determined. Nothing will ever hold you back once you've made up your mind and this seems to be the case during this month.

The pattern made by the stars seems to suggest that you're very one-sided and only interested in the professional part to life. You may be socializing but it's likely to be with workmates or with someone you believe can help you up the ladder of success. Other sides to life are going to be totally deserted and there are going to be some loud complaints from loved ones, especially if you have a loving mate who is beginning to get a little fed up with sitting alone at night – and who can blame them. Try to reach a happy medium, Scorpio, although I realize it's not easy for your sign. This is the best way to go during July and if you don't, you'll be storing up a great deal of trouble.

1 MONDAY It's imperative you don't take any chances with paperwork – it would be all too easy for you to misinterpret anything you read. Travel may be complicated, too, so check all arrangements and timetables and in this way you'll save yourself a great deal of unnecessary aggravation. Romantically, someone could be out to deceive you, so be suspicious.

2 TUESDAY It seems very likely that you have tolerated a great deal over recent days in the hope that a problematical domestic situation would eventually prove to be worthwhile. Today, however, you realize this will never be, so it's better to abandon hope and make the necessary adjustments than to keep struggling on fruitlessly. In order to keep in a positive mind, dwell on your successes.

3 WEDNESDAY Over the next couple of days you're likely to be making interesting contacts who can no doubt help you, not just professionally but also in your personal life. If you work as part of a team there may very well be a breakthrough or some excitement. If you're visiting a club in your spare time, fascinating people will enter your life.

4 THURSDAY Some heavy rivalry or opposition seems to be throwing you off balance and causing distraction in your daily routine. The wisest thing you can do is to size up the competition and decide exactly how you can launch your own assault. You could very well find that surprise tactics will catch others off guard and lead to a relatively easy, but well deserved, triumph.

5 FRIDAY The best advice that can be given today is that a united front will do much to bring some semblance of order to cash arrangements. Remember, though, that some jobs are best performed in private, or without the help of anyone else.

However, on this occasion, a public display of your joint strength, enthusiasm and vigour will certainly go a long way to enhancing your image.

6 SATURDAY The stars could lead you to be careless or slap-dash. You find concentration elusive and the thing to do is to spend your day putting the finishing touches to work, rather than starting anything new. Don't allow others to bully you into making world shattering decisions as yet.

7 SUNDAY Today Mercury will be moving into the water sign of Cancer and that's the area of your chart devoted to socializing, children and casual romance. Some of you will be drawn to intellectual pastimes, whilst others will want to be more flippant and let off a bit of steam. Whichever avenue you decide to take will be all right by the stars.

8 MONDAY You may find older or more experienced people a drag on your progress today; for you their advice seems old fashioned and their attitude negative – and you could be right. The best course to steer is one where you are master of your own fate and in this way you will be unable to blame anybody else.

9 TUESDAY There's a definite slowing down of your progress which is no bad thing, because this will allow you time to think things through, particularly those fiddling little details that you so often ignore. The chance to get out locally with friends should be snapped up this evening because you'll be in the mood for socializing.

Monthly and Daily Guides: July

10 WEDNESDAY Today is the day of the new Moon and it falls in the water sign of Cancer. Whenever there is a new Moon we can all push ahead with our secret desires and this is a time for you to do just that, they will materialize in the not too distant future.

11 THURSDAY Today Venus will be moving into Virgo and that's the area of your chart devoted to friendship, team effort, and new ambitions. Should you have a Virgo in your life, they're going to be very 'lovey-dovey' during the next few weeks or so, so that if you need any extra help or assistance from them, they'll be only too glad to help you out.

12 FRIDAY The planets provide you with a wonderful day for making world-shattering decisions because you are able to see so clearly. Many of you may also decide to take on a more serious view of a current relationship; you're not exactly ready to march up the aisle, but you are prepared to let the other person know exactly how you feel.

13 SATURDAY Today you really can't rely on anybody; others are elusive, hard to get hold of and downright indecisive. Get out your independent muscles and flex them as much as possible, basically because you're going to need them, if nothing else. Lastly, other people have some pretty outrageous ideas which may seem practical to them but, after giving them a listen, you'll realize that these are just pipe dreams and you won't want anything to do with them – very wise.

14 SUNDAY Today Mars will be moving into Leo and that's the area of your chart devoted to work, which is going to be pretty hectic over the next couple of days or so. It might be a good idea to rest up from time to time because you could overstretch yourself and that is not the ideal thing to do. If you have a Leo in your life they could be quite impatient.

15 MONDAY Today the stars suggest that it is important for you to review, or maybe even renegotiate, personal or family arrangements which seem to be falling apart in record time. Why continue to toe the line in a situation which is tailored to the demands of other people? This is not a time to forget your own needs.

16 TUESDAY This is a time for focussing on what you want instead of providing props for your nearest and dearest. The planets suggest you're beginning at least to recognize your own needs as well as those of your partner or loved ones. Remember, if you are true to others, first and foremost you must be true to yourself.

17 WEDNESDAY This is a time when you must not lose sight of your own aims and ambitions just because you're expected to contribute more, perhaps unreasonably, to a partnership or a family matter. You have every right to expect a fair deal in return for the heavy demands which have been made upon you lately.

18 THURSDAY You could use this day for assessing your progress to date and working out exactly what you want in the future. That's not to say you shouldn't have some fun and, in fact, friends who live close by will make sure that you do. However, don't expect to find serious romance at the moment.

♏

19 FRIDAY There is a possibility that you may gain from a calculated risk that you took recently. Certainly, money is well-starred today so you may have a happy surprise. If you do, don't spend it all at once – you are sure to regret it later.

20 SATURDAY This is a day when you really can't believe everything friends and acquaintances, or contacts, say. Not that they are necessarily out to deceive you, but they could very well have their wires crossed and pass on wrong information which, if you act upon it, could lead to disaster. If you've anything arranged for this evening it wouldn't do any harm to do a little bit of double checking.

21 SUNDAY There's a possibility that you'll be a little bit muddled. Fortunately you're also at your most inspired and creative and if you need these talents for work you will certainly shine. However, it would be a good idea to put paperwork to one side for a while because mistakes could be expensive at a later date. This evening, if you're feeling at all jaded, be strong and turn down invitations for having fun.

22 MONDAY Today Mercury will be moving into the fiery sign of Leo, the area of your chart devoted to work, so you can expect paperwork and documents to be extremely important in your working life and, if you're lucky, you may be asked to go on a trip which could be quite glamorous. Accept all that is on offer in the working area of life and you won't go far wrong.

23 TUESDAY The stars today will be kind to those of you involved in buying, selling, advertising or the media. And it's good for other Scorpios who are determined to 'bargain hunt' because you'll be buying something of value at an unbelievably good price. Romantically, it's a time for brief encounters.

24 WEDNESDAY Today is the day of the full Moon and it falls in the sign of Aquarius, which is devoted to the home, so it looks as if you're going to be spending a good deal more of your time there and that is going to please other people no end. Mind you, because of the full Moon, it's also a good time for putting the finishing touches to work, as well as getting in some extra rest – that won't do you any harm at all.

25 THURSDAY You need to take care where romance is concerned over the next couple of days or so, mainly due to the fact that other people will be devious and out to pull the wool over your eyes. If you're not careful you could become seriously involved with a person already engaged or married and this, of course, will be storing up hurt for the future, so don't allow your romantic heart to carry you off into the wide blue yonder.

26 FRIDAY Financially some good news seems to be in the pipeline and this boosts your ego no end. However, do make sure that you don't spend it before the money is safely tucked away in your bank. You know what you're like, any chance to over-indulge is always snapped up in record time, but if you do so now, you'll certainly rue this particular day.

27 SATURDAY Today the stars suggest you'll feel at your happiest moving out of the driving seat and letting others take over for a while, because you need time to think things through before you go any further. However, don't push yourself to achieve when most of the signposts in life point towards a more reflective period.

♏

28 SUNDAY Today it's important that you find out what's going on behind the scenes in every area. The stars suggest that you involve yourself in a little research and investigation in order to find out the true facts behind situations. If you rush in where angels fear to tread, you will almost certainly live to regret it.

29 MONDAY Well, Scorpio, generally you are very reluctant to move on from old contacts, but really the time has come for you to cut loose from those who are holding you back from success. Today, the stars will reveal that not everyone is on your wavelength, or capable of being as honest and as straightforward as you are.

30 TUESDAY An ideal day for extracting a few favours, making your feelings known to that special person in your life and even trying some different and exciting new pastimes. You may be surprised at your behaviour which is all to the good, because too often other people take you for granted and so if you're surprised, imagine how they feel.

31 WEDNESDAY Today a very special friend could spin a pleasant surprise which may eventually result in an exciting change in your life. Work also has an exhilarating feel about it. Perhaps a big deal is about to be struck or there are promotion prospects in the air.

AUGUST

The Sun will be drifting along in the sign of Leo until 22 August and that, of course, is the zenith point of your chart. You'll become very 'one-pointed' and extremely ambitious, so heaven help anybody who wants to get in your way. Do think of other people, though. You will be making enemies if you don't and you really don't want that.

On 23 August, the Sun will be moving into Virgo, the area of your chart devoted to team effort, friends and acquaintances, so do not be too frightened to ask for any kind of advice. We all need some help from time to time and this happens to be your time; it is no reflection on your abilities in any way, shape or form.

Mercury remains in Leo for the first five days, still making it a good time for communications and minor changes. On 6 August Mercury will be moving into the earthy sign of Virgo. Welcome invitations from friends may be in the offing and there may also be the opportunity to travel on business. Both should be considered.

Venus will be in Virgo for the first six days, and if you have a member of this sign in your life they'll be willing to help you out in any way they can. Friends, acquaintances and team effort and the word 'cooperation' suddenly become extremely important and you, for one, see the value of this. From 7 August Venus will be moving through Libra. Normally you are honest and reliable when it comes to relationships, but you may now be feeling the temptation to stray. Resist this, because it will only lead to trouble.

Mars will be in Leo until 29 August and that, of course, is the zenith point of your chart, so once more everything is focused on hard work. However, if you find that you're getting too tired, then shelve things temporarily because you could become inefficient and that would go against the old Scorpio grain, wouldn't it?

The pattern made by the stars seems to suggest that you'll be starting many new projects, relationships and ideas during

Monthly and Daily Guides: August

this period, but you may lack 'follow through'. That could be your Achilles heel, so make sure that you employ tenacity and endurance – you've plenty of the stuff when you need it, so make sure that you use it effectively.

1 THURSDAY There's no point in continuing to glance over your shoulders, Scorpio, when it seems there's so much for you to look forward to in the future. The stars are attempting to persuade you to shake loose from the remnants of an old life and have confidence in a new idea or project. The more you are ready to take any minor risk, the more likely it is that your performance will draw an audience.

2 FRIDAY If you are to keep up with your current rate of growth in life, you need to examine the state of your bank account. The webs we weave when we enter joint arrangements and throw in our lot with other people can either create a strong safety net or a tangled interplay which threatens to trap even the most adventurous member of your sign. So think carefully about reaching any agreements.

3 SATURDAY At first glance love affairs and creative enterprises look good, but a second look reveals a power struggle which leads to a conflict developing, either sexually or financially. On the most intimate level it could lead to an unhealthy situation where one is used to gain the other, and it may mean problems in your private life as a result of a lack of one or the other. Things need sorting out fast.

4 SUNDAY The most important matters right now are those connected with relationships; this is due to the fact that you might be getting a sneaky feeling that you have been living on borrowed time where a partner or associate is concerned. There really isn't any reason for you to put up with somebody else's heavy demands.

5 MONDAY A recent drama and aggravations connected with intimate relationships may have left you feeling jaded or slightly below par. What you need at this moment is to put some order back into your life and the sooner the better. Boring though it may appear, sorting out practical matters will renew your commitment to yourself and your future.

6 TUESDAY Today Mercury will be moving into Virgo and that's the area of your chart devoted to friends, team effort, and people in general. Just for once it might be a good idea to put other people first. Not only will this gain you recognition but it is, quite frankly, the right thing to do.

7 WEDNESDAY If you are an artistic Scorpio, then you need to reconnect with your artistry and this may mean you will have to throw out some rather limiting ideas. Perhaps because you have been recently concerned with such serious ambitions, some of the sparkle you normally reserve for those closest to you, may have been missing. The next few days will offer you the perfect opportunity to drop this self-imposed level of duty and follow your own emotions.

8 THURSDAY Today is the day of the new Moon and it occurs at the zenith point of your chart in the fiery sign of Leo. Therefore, where work and ambitions are concerned there are sure to be changes, maybe new people entering your company or your firm. Do not view them with suspicion; instead,

Monthly and Daily Guides: August

try to make a friend of them. As always, new Moons are a great time for fresh starts.

9 FRIDAY Making plans and protecting your position is absolutely essential if you are to move on to a more successful level of life. Others don't necessarily possess your principles or your intuition so you must not let them overturn your plans, however forcefully they may try to. Even though you are a water sign, you can't expect to live your life in a swimming pool – tangible reward for your talents is needed practically, but also as proof of your ability.

10 SATURDAY You may find your practical sense of reality dissolving before your very eyes. You seem to be experiencing a greater urge to get closer in your relationship, yet finding the right way of directing the whole proceedings still remains a mystery. Don't lie awake worrying about this, the stars will soon let you know when your instincts and the time are right.

11 SUNDAY Today could bring some kind of challenge and this will raise your vitality level and make you more in tune with what is really important. Certainly it looks as if a difficult chapter in your life, in which you have felt lost, is closing and being replaced with increased confidence. Your ability to be successful is not a matter of winning or losing, but living your life imaginatively.

12 MONDAY You seem to be in the spotlight and this suggests you could be raking in the rewards of past struggles and efforts on the working front. Alternatively, some of you may be lucky enough to win a small amount of money. If so, don't blow the whole lot in celebration – that's not the clever thing to do. If you're in a relationship, you'll find your partner is in a particularly warm and affectionate mood and differences can be forgotten.

13 TUESDAY There's no point in trying to get through to other people. The best thing to do is to struggle on alone until the current atmosphere changes. There's one positive aspect, though, which is that the special person in your life may be in a sentimental and romantic mood this evening and, if so, you'll no doubt be delighted because this fits in with your own mood.

14 WEDNESDAY Today, wherever you go, you'll find them rolling in the aisles, and just being around you will be better than taking a fortnight's holiday. Summer's not a bad time for romance, just as long as you're not expecting to meeting Romeo/Juliet and can content yourself with a human being with all the faults and failings which that entails.

15 THURSDAY Recent financial complications are likely to be a thing of the past, and problems will be melting away as the days and weeks pass. No doubt this is especially welcome news for those who work in the monied professions, because if this applies to you then one drama follows on the heels of yet another. All Scorpios can afford to push their luck where cash matters are concerned.

16 FRIDAY Today you could develop a love at first sight for something and spend before you've had time to think. One lapse of extravagance you can probably afford, but you must make sure that this inclination evaporates once the day is through, or you'll certainly live to regret it.

♏

Monthly and Daily Guides: August

17 SATURDAY There's certainly some good news if you work creatively, or if you rely on your intuitions. You're sensitive to your environment and company too, so rude or crude people will offend, and unpleasant or dingy surroundings will bring you down. So, clearly, this is a time to be picky when it comes to deciding what you're going to do socially and who you're going to spend your time with.

18 SUNDAY It's a good time for sorting out anything connected with your social life or with children; decisions made on behalf of offspring will certainly be the right ones. If, on the other hand, you are fancy free, you'll be in the mood for flirting but for heaven's sake don't allow anyone to take you too seriously, because you could unintentionally hurt them and regret it at a later date.

19 MONDAY In the long run nothing you face should be so challenging that you can't find a solution, but thinking matters through will take time. For this reason you must make your obligations your first priority, even if it means temporarily sidelining certain other ideas, projects or even people.

20 TUESDAY From now on, for a couple of days, you must double check travel plans and paperwork and make sure that you express yourself clearly, because it's all too easy for other people to get the wrong end of the stick. If misunderstandings do occur, it is imperative that you sit down immediately and sort them out before they become exaggerated beyond all belief.

21 WEDNESDAY Don't be surprised if you have to change your social and romantic plans at the last moment. Naturally, this will prove to be disappointing, but at a later date you'll come to realize that this occurred for a reason and in the end things worked out for the best.

22 THURSDAY Today is the day of the full Moon and it occurs in the airy sign of Aquarius, the area of your chart devoted to property, family and the home, where there could be some discord going on at this time. If you're in the process of trying to purchase property, don't do anything on this particular day because if you do, you could come severely unstuck.

23 FRIDAY Today the Sun will be moving into Virgo and that's the area of your chart devoted to friends, team effort and acquaintances. You suddenly become much more gregarious and sociable and this helps you to forget any worries that you might have. Be prepared to accept all invitations, no matter how peculiar or 'different' – you could do with a bit of a shaking up.

24 SATURDAY You could certainly be a great deal better off when this day is over. You'll be quick to recognize financial opportunities and will snap them up before other people have had time to draw breath. Meetings with financial people will go well so, Scorpio, you've every reason for feeling confidence. Put those insecurities away and push into life.

25 SUNDAY This is obviously a time for pushing ahead with all that is important to you, because you will find yourself repeatedly in a position where you can turn the world around on its head. Romantically, if you are unattached, there's a strong chance of meeting someone special. Alternatively, if you're already in a relationship, you may be prepared to take it that step forward, and engagements and marriages are certainly well-starred.

26 MONDAY This could very well be a day of brief encounters, some of which will be of a romantic nature, but others could result in chance meetings with people who can help you with your financial and professional difficulties. Take advantage of this day by making sure you are looking good and keeping a high profile. There's no point in hiding your light under a bushel because other people simply aren't psychic.

27 TUESDAY Today you can't altogether rely on the words of the friends, contacts or acquaintances. Certainly, they mean well and intend to fulfil their promises to you, but circumstances which crop up quite suddenly in their lives may make it difficult for them to do so. Be as philosophical as you usually are and whatever you do, don't bear grudges.

28 WEDNESDAY Other people in your life, at work and at home, could be deliberately perverse or even rebellious. What to do? I'm not suggesting you ignore them, simply go about your own business in your usual quiet fashion and, if they want to throw tantrums, sulk or be difficult, allow them to do so. Once they've got this out of their system, they may become more approachable and human once more.

29 THURSDAY Hold on to possessions because some unlikely person may remove them for you. Double check change when visiting the shops and, in fact, don't take any kind of chance with your hard-earned cash because you can't afford to lose any.

♏

30 FRIDAY You could be warm, sunny and even more boisterous than is usually the case. You'll feel ready to take on the whole wide world with one hand tied behind your back. If you have anything important that you want to tackle today, don't hesitate for a moment, this is a time for action.

31 SATURDAY Well, Scorpio, the rest of us usually know that you're after something when you put on the charm, but we still can't help falling under your spell anyway. This is particularly true today, so whatever or whoever you want, you're sure to win. You could also be raking in some extra cash or maybe given a chance to prove yourself.

SEPTEMBER

The Sun will be coasting along in Virgo up until 22 September, and that is the area of your chart devoted to friends and acquaintances, as well as your ambitions. If you work as part of a team you'll be doing exceptionally well, and this is certainly a time for pushing ahead with all you want out of life, so don't let the grass grow underneath your feet.

On 23 September, the Sun will be moving into Libra and that's a rather hidden part of your chart, so you're going to have a couple of days or so when you should be using your intuition and your instincts rather than that busy, active head. There's a lot going on around you but maybe you're totally oblivious to it and that would be a pity, because it could mean you're missing out.

Mercury will be situated in Libra all month, churning up your subconscious. You may have a sudden desire to get on the telephone to someone you haven't spoken to for simply ages and, if so, don't let anything hold you back. Go with your intuition, no matter what it is telling you, though it's unlikely to be affecting your love life too much.

Venus will be in Scorpio from the 8th and that, of course, is your sign. Maybe you should hang fire on anything that's important until this date because once Venus enters your sign you look good, feel good and nobody can resist you, believe me. Those of you who are fancy free may very well meet somebody important around this time so you need to keep your eyes peeled. Conversely, if you're already in a relationship you've got to resist the temptation to stray, which will be strong.

Mars is located in Virgo, the area of your chart devoted to friends and acquaintances, and there's a distinct possibility that you could be too sharp and abrasive with those old friends of yours. Naturally, they'll probably understand, but if you do this too much they may get so fed up with you that they cut you out of their lives completely and that would be a big pity, which you will regret.

The pattern made by the stars this month is a scattered one which means that you may concentrate on one side of life for a while and then change over to another side, but at least by doing this it's quite likely that you will prevent yourself from becoming too bored. What other people make of it though is particularly relevant and you'll have to wait and see.

1 SUNDAY You rarely make a fuss about anything you do, but you seem particularly quiet at the moment. This doesn't mean there's nothing going on – far from it. You're busy hatching financial schemes which are sure to pay off in the near future. This is one of those rare times when you begin to realize you have an awful lot to offer the rest of the world. Don't be afraid to show off your considerable talents.

2 MONDAY Don't allow your brain to move faster than your body, otherwise you could be in for one or two mishaps or clumsy words spoken which necessitate apologies. Apart from this, you're in tip-top, sparkling form, rushing around galvanizing everyone else into action with your energy and determination. You're even more prepared to be experimental in all areas of life, so this evening could be extremely interesting and certainly a time for getting out and about and meeting new people.

3 TUESDAY You're the kind of person who loves to make changes but you like to create them too, and feel uncomfortable when others are doing this for you, which could be the case today. Think about their suggestions and then I think you'll find you'll get excited. If you have been recently stuck in the past, this is an ideal time for shaking off this mood and getting out and having some fun.

4 WEDNESDAY You're likely to be experiencing electrifying impulses where your cash flow is concerned. You sense that matters are going to change and they are, but don't worry, this will certainly be for the best, so in the meantime try to be patient. The stars are giving you plenty of charisma, inspiration and creativity so you've got loads of confidence.

5 THURSDAY You seem to be leaning so heavily on someone they're in danger of falling over. Get a grip on yourself, Scorpio, make a conscious effort to stand on your own two feet because right now others have got quite enough problems of their own. Cashwise, the urge to splurge is upon you, so beware.

6 FRIDAY You seem to be blowing up minor problems into major disasters. Calm down, Scorpio, and try to take some time to sit down and think things through. This way you'll make life easier for yourself, as well as those closest to you. Having done this, you'll find it a great deal easier to talk common sense into somebody close.

7 SATURDAY Today is the day of the new Moon and it occurs in the earthy sign of Virgo, the area of your chart devoted to friends and contacts, and these people are likely to be springing one or two surprises. This evening get out and about because you're likely to be introduced to a new circle of friends, and they will be in your life for some considerable while. As always, new Moons suggest new beginnings for all.

8 SUNDAY Today Venus will be moving into your own sign and that's the area of your chart which represents all of your own self-interests. My goodness me, you're going to be looking good, feeling good, you will be at your most charming and attracting admirers in their droves over the next couple of days. If you have decided to become engaged or married, you've certainly been a very clever Scorpio indeed. Congratulations.

9 MONDAY It could be that other people are too carefree today, maybe too slapdash and optimistic. Certainly the mood is a pleasant one, but it wouldn't be a good idea to take any advice from them because it's highly unlikely that they've really done their homework. Be self-reliant.

10 TUESDAY For some reason you're not your usual well-balanced self and are entertaining high hopes for a new relationship where a pet project is concerned. If this is to succeed, it's important to remain objective otherwise you could finish up disappointed and that would be a pity.

11 WEDNESDAY Self-indulgence seems to be rife at this time and there's no reason why you shouldn't spoil yourself just a little, but do try to keep this within the bounds of reason, otherwise you're likely to have your bank manager in floods of tears. Those closest to you are in a happy-go-lucky mood.

12 THURSDAY You are, of course, a cherishing person but sometimes it's all too easy for others to take advantage of you. This certainly seems to be the case where family are concerned at the moment, so this is a period when you should consider putting your foot down firmly. Your energy levels may also tend to be a little lower than usual, so why don't you rest up this evening?

13 FRIDAY Avoid important decisions or moves for the time being because you really can't see the proverbial wood for the trees. You have plenty of time later on in the month for pushing ahead. In the meantime, make plans but don't act. Usually you know exactly who and what you want and are rarely in two minds about anything, but today you seem to be dithering.

14 SATURDAY Today Mercury will be going into retrograde movement, so from hereon in people born under the sign of Gemini or Virgo could be extremely obstructive. Not only that, but paperwork and travelling could also be unnecessarily complicated, so try to stay away from these sides to life for the time being.

Monthly and Daily Guides: September

15 SUNDAY Where work is concerned you can push ahead without fear of rejection or confusion. Advantages which come to you completely out of the blue can be snapped up without worry and they'll work for you. As far as professional money is concerned, the next few weeks will be decidedly rewarding as well as fulfilling.

16 MONDAY There's a possibility that recently you have been struggling to find solutions to problems but they have remained elusive. However, now the planets are in the right position to encourage your common sense, and because of this, the answers will leap into your brain and you can't think why you hadn't found them before now.

17 TUESDAY Because complications and difficulties connected with family and property slowly begin to melt away over the next few days, you'll be able to release negative feelings which have been troubling you in these two areas. Furthermore, opportunities connected with work could come unexpectedly.

18 WEDNESDAY Today you become typically Scorpionic, being perhaps more jealous and tense and certainly possessive. Be warned, too, that excesses will hold strong appeal for you and if you're not careful they will make an enormous hole in your bank account. On the other hand, if you work creatively, you'll certainly be bringing a smile to your bank manager's face.

19 THURSDAY Today you are advised to be as independent as possible because other people seem to be depressed, dejected and very negative. Being the sensitive person you are, their mood could very easily rub off on you, so see what you can do to isolate yourself, get on with what needs to be done and make sure you get plenty of rest this evening.

20 FRIDAY Slowly over the next couple of days cash matters will be improving in leaps and bounds. There's no need to worry any longer, but be ready to take on board profitable ideas which can enrich you in a big way. Even if you have been snowed under with cash problems, you will still be given a chance to show that gentleness and patience provide you with power.

21 SATURDAY Today is the day of the full Moon and it occurs in the water sign of Pisces, the area of your chart devoted to children, creativity and casual romance. However, complications are bound to set in so face them bravely, but then again what else would you do?

22 SUNDAY The best thing to do today, Scorpio, is to pace yourself because you've got so much to do. Therefore, turn your attention to that which is of the utmost importance and leave anything else on the side for the time being. Your imagination is likely to run riot this evening and exaggerate problems beyond all belief – you have been warned.

23 MONDAY You should still be feeling more relaxed and tolerant, particularly where others are concerned. Cash difficulties will continue to improve in leaps and bounds and the stars will continue to show their gentleness and patience and provide you with power. Nevertheless, you must still be alert to the possibility of profitable ideas.

24 TUESDAY The Sun has now moved into Libra and that's a rather secretive area to your chart, so over the next few days or so you could become positively 'psychic'. You always have a 'feel' for what is about to occur and this is heightened during this time – others may even think you are being very spooky. Working in the background will be a good idea.

25 WEDNESDAY Not only should your feelings guide you, those instincts could deal with power struggles more handily than pure logic. If partners don't respond to reason or gentle persuasion, just give them time. Very soon both your confidence and control will have returned, leaving former critics trying to keep up with you.

26 THURSDAY Ironically, in at least one instance, exchanges transform previously tense situations and could even bring closer personal ties, which can't be bad. While cash matters cannot be forgotten completely, decide nothing until a few days have passed, as dramatic developments are more than you can take for the time being.

27 FRIDAY Workwise make sure you draw other people's attention to your talents today, particularly if you're out of work. A new phase in your family life seems to be dawning and you should feel free to make any changes you want to at home, because they're sure to prove to be a success in the end. Romantically, you may be considering reviving an old romance, but do think twice, or even three times.

28 SATURDAY Today the stars will be opening up your mind to new ideas and methods of work. Communications will be important so don't ignore telephone messages or letters, because to do so could very well mean that you'll miss out in some way, and that would never do. Get out this evening because you're going to be lively company.

29 SUNDAY Friends and acquaintances are in a caring, nurturing and loving mood; if you need some advice or comfort don't hesitate to go to them because they will most certainly not let you down. Romantically, you could very well meet someone new.

30 MONDAY You will miss that feeling of taking one step forward and two steps back. From now on, all areas of your life can be lived up to your highest expectations. If you have experienced a lack of communication or problems with close relationships, this day will bring with it a fresh start when you can become a good deal closer. Yes, you are cementing the bonds of love that you have recently established; not only that, you also find that you have learned a great deal from past mistakes and that's good.

OCTOBER

The Sun this month will be floating along in the airy sign of Libra, and that's a rather secretive part of your chart. It represents your instincts, your intuition, work that's going on behind the scenes and sometimes your insecurities. Luckily, Scorpios are usually born with innate confidence so, no doubt, you can sort this out without any difficulty at all.

On 24 October, the Sun will be moving into your own sign, so you look good, you feel good and you're not going to allow anyone to pin you down – and why should you? This is a part of the year when you can please yourself, as well as get

Monthly and Daily Guides: October

your own way. However, don't forget to turn on the charm, as it doesn't hurt to be polite and considerate of other people as I'm quite sure you know.

All month Mercury is in a changeable mood. From 2 to 10 October it is in the earth sign of Virgo before then moving on into the sign of Libra. However, during the first couple of days it is in retrograde movement so avoid any important travelling, paperwork and legal matters because if you get involved with those you're going to get yourself into one hell of a mess.

Luckily, after 6 October, and for the remainder of the month, Mercury is behaving itself, so little for you to worry about there.

Venus is good news, because it is in your sign for the entire month. Mind you, perhaps the best time for pushing ahead with everything that is important to you is during the first week. This is because Venus starts to play up on the 10th and goes into retrograde movement, where it stays for the remainder of this month. Venus in retrograde can mean that other people will be either trying to avoid you, or giving you advice which is totally wrong, even though their intentions are good. One way or another you'll wish that you had relied on your excellent judgement, and if you can do this, there will be nothing for you to fret about.

Mars is situated in the earthy sign of Virgo up until 15 October, so there's a short period here when your male friends may be important. All contacts and acquaintances could be a little bit stressed, bad tempered and uncooperative, but luckily you are an extremely independent person, so you can cope without any help from anybody else, thank you very much.

On the 16th, Mars will be moving into Libra where it stays for the remainder of the month. There's something going on here, Scorpio – I don't know what you're getting up to. Mars, of course, is the planet of sex but it seems to be rather hidden. Are you being naughty? In other words, if you've got a mate, you may be being unfaithful – it's very unusual but even so it's a possibility that's worth pointing out just in case you even begin to think about. In a word – don't.

The pattern made by the stars seems to be a rather scattered one which is unusual for you, because you're very good at centralizing your activities and doing things well and thoroughly before you move on to anything else. However, do remember there are quite a few planets in retrograde movement, so you mustn't take anything for granted. The best thing you can do is to refer to the Daily Guides so that you are able to sidestep any difficulty – it shouldn't be hard for a strong person like you.

1 TUESDAY You begin the month feeling sparkling and confident; you're certainly going to be full of the joys of living. Wherever you go, other people seem to be tripping over their feet in a rush to do you favours, asking you to join them socially, and flattering your ego to such a degree that you could be impossible to live with by the time this evening comes. Never mind, Scorpio, bask in all of this popularity, but make sure you give back a little in return, because this is something you occasionally forget to do.

2 WEDNESDAY Today's aspects will certainly help to calm troubled waters. On the other hand, if a partner, be it professional or personal, is unwilling to be more open-minded and flexible, it may well be the time to find a more deserving companion. Right now, a major upheaval may seem the only logical response to a problem, but very soon the groundwork will be done, and you will then be able to take your time to ring one or two changes.

3 THURSDAY You're certainly going to be making an impact on the world at large, but you must pick the best area in which to concentrate all your efforts. The stars suggest that you're preparing for one of the most important periods of the year. What's more, as a very strong and determined sign, you don't always welcome the thought of moving around, or even travelling, unless you deem it to be necessary. However, you can rest assured because with so much on your side, you can't put a foot wrong, unless, of course, you really try hard.

4 FRIDAY We all need other people at some point in life and this is most certainly a time for remembering this. Other people are lucky and imaginative and will be able to give you a fresh slant on all problems, as well as contributing a great deal to your social life this evening. If you've had your eye on a member of the opposite sex for some while now, this is a great time for making that move.

5 SATURDAY You really do seem to be spoiled for good aspects on this day. For you, it's a lucky time for dealing with matters related to education or affairs abroad. Sports, children and romance all have a happy glow about them, and so if there's something you want to change or talk through in these areas, put aside excuses and jump in head first, as you sometimes do. Just for a change, you'll be saying the right thing at the right time.

6 SUNDAY Today is the day of the new Moon and it occurs in Libra. You're feeling quietly confident about all areas of life and you're not too anxious to make a big display of this fact. You will quietly get on with what you've got to do, which will at a later date prove to be extremely successful. As always, with new Moons it's a great time for making fresh starts and this one is no exception. If you're not satisfied with something, change it, the stars will guarantee a degree of success.

7 MONDAY Fortunately, Mercury has now resumed direct movement, so from hereon in anything connected with paperwork, legal affairs, travelling or people in your circle who are born under Virgo or Gemini will be extremely lucky for you. Don't hesitate to make any important moves in connection with these sides to life because you'll be sorry if you don't.

8 TUESDAY This is certainly not a day for asserting yourself where officials and bureaucrats are concerned because, if you do, you're likely to get your wrists slapped. Stick to the letter of the law and catch up on routine work which has, no doubt, been neglected, even if it's only around the house. Also, try to find a way to truly relax this evening, remember it's the company you keep which will please, rather than any particular activity.

9 WEDNESDAY Today you seem to be in the limelight and lapping up all the attention, which no doubt is deserved. If you want to present changes to your family, your boss or to that special person in your life, you couldn't have a better time because they'll be able to see your point of view and will agree with you 100 percent, Scorpio. You can certainly get your own way on this particular day. Don't let it go to waste.

Monthly and Daily Guides: October

10 THURSDAY Unfortunately, Venus decides to go into retrograde movement and because of this other people may either try to avoid you, or will perhaps be lacking in any kind of support that you might need. Nevertheless, just as long as you remain polite and courteous to them and get on with your own business, they'll see the light and will probably be making a big fuss of you later on.

11 FRIDAY Oh dear! Now Saturn has decided to go into retrograde movement. Saturn represents the area of your chart devoted to the mind and short journeys and also to the affairs of brothers and sisters. Any, or all, of these could become complicated and difficult to gauge, but luckily with your determination you will win through. You must not trample all over other people's sensibilities or ideas, though; at least give them a listen so that you can stay on the right side of them. I'm not suggesting that you crawl, which would be expecting too much from a proud Scorpio, but even so, just remember their right to what they think.

12 SATURDAY After a lot of dithering, which perhaps has caused you to say the wrong thing at the wrong time, this could very well be a day for mopping up. It's possible that a number of things have come to light over recent days and now you can act upon them. However, your real success and profit comes from self-evaluation, for if you value your own worth you will have everyone else believing in you, too, and that can't be bad.

13 SUNDAY Today the stars are on great form and seem to suggest you can look forward to favourable changes within the family and at home, which will have a positive effect on your life, as well as your work. It seems that an unconventional approach may be the only way to resolve a long-standing problem, so say what you mean, mean what you say and things will definitely improve.

14 MONDAY Today the stars suggest that the better you feel within yourself, in a relationship, the more progress you'll make in other areas, and it's very much a case of putting your personal life first for a change. Naturally, you are fiercely ambitious, being a Scorpio, but there are occasions when other considerations need your attention and this happens to be one of them. Try to arrange something special for the person most important to you and this will provide you with a chance to relax, which is much needed right now.

15 TUESDAY You, as an ambitious Scorpio, like to be on top, but unless you control your cash flow, rivals may undermine you. In the past, restrictions seem to have thwarted your progress in all directions but life needn't be like that on this particular day. Harness the energies the stars are providing and push forward, and remember you're an asset to anything connected with your job.

16 WEDNESDAY Today Mars will be moving into the secretive area of your chart in Libra and because of this you may be inwardly feeling tense, short-tempered and ready to explode if somebody as much as looks at you in the wrong way. Keep your head down wherever you are and don't even try to be sociable, but at least stay polite so that you don't create bad feeling.

Monthly and Daily Guides: October

17 THURSDAY Today is the time for putting your own house in order. If you don't, you'll set an uneasy tone for the remainder of the year. Try to avoid making arrangements which mean heavy financial commitments. If there are already plans in motion, be ready for certain setbacks. Involve others in your plans, such as relatives and loved ones: if you have a heart to heart with your loved ones, you'll be drawing strength from this and feeling more relaxed.

18 FRIDAY You can't rely on other people for literally anything; they are confused, muddled and dreamy, so as long as you stay your usual independent self you'll be able to sidestep potential problems. This evening, on no account allow yourself to become emotionally carried away; you may be able to convince yourself that a sexual attraction means a great deal and this could lead to hurt in the future.

19 SATURDAY You're fairly confident today but please don't get carried away or believe that minimum effort will bring maximum results, because it won't. There are several unlikely schemes in the air and you'd be better off concentrating on more worthwhile projects. Although what happens in the future isn't entirely reliant on what you do right now, you must respond correctly and open your eyes to certain home truths.

20 SUNDAY There's a happy relaxed feel about this particular day, as a few understandings have been reached. And, if life or love has lost lustre, the stars today will soon put it back. What's more, you'll be sensing a favourable change in the wind. Your luck is certainly in, but there are risky plans you want to get off the ground, so make sure you do so under favourable conditions.

21 MONDAY Today is the day of the full Moon and it occurs in the fiery sign of Aries. Be particularly scrupulous in work matters today. To madly rush into things will only put you back a long way. Also, don't be surprised if a colleague is in a bad temper – just don't take them seriously.

22 TUESDAY You're very good at helping other people but now it's your turn to be on the receiving end of others' time and energy. If you start to assert yourself a little more, you'll be gaining greater respect for yourself, and will be opening up good opportunities too. It may be best to keep plans in reserve and play safe. The longer you hold your cards close to your chest, the better your chances of hitting the jackpot at a later date.

23 WEDNESDAY From now on your progress in all areas of life should be much smoother and more successful. Physically, you'll begin to blossom, too, mainly because you're feeling so much more relaxed. Tension and stress are always the worst things for our looks, regardless of whether we're male or female, so take a look in the mirror and you'll probably see somebody who looks at least five years younger.

24 THURSDAY Today the Sun will be moving into your sign and so from hereon in the stars are providing you with a period when you can push ahead with everything that is important to you. Even physically you sparkle, dazzle, are witty and others clamber around. Certainly your social life is going to be busy and so if you happen to be single, there are going to be lots of chances for romance, so stay alert.

♏

25 FRIDAY Today the stars seem to be preparing you for a new stage in life, but it's pointless taking this for granted, at least for another couple of weeks or so. This time you'll be able to see whether your ideas are successful, or whether you need to get back to the drawing board and re-think. The most important thing to do is to be objective: the stars suggest that the more impartial you are, the greater your performance will be.

26 SATURDAY Very soon you will find out how far you have come and just how much further you need to travel. You seem to be learning a great deal at this time, but even so the planets are making you somewhat impressionable and easily deceived, particularly where work matters are concerned, so you need to take care if you're in an ambitious mood. Concentrate on people and places who are at a distance.

27 SUNDAY You really must go out of your way to be a little more giving and thoughtful. People who are important in your life seem to be ready to start talking problems through. Luckily, you are the sort of person who thrives on confrontation and so now you have a chance to explain your feelings and say exactly what has been bothering you recently.

28 MONDAY Today the stars will help to improve your self-expression and you'll be using charm rather than force, persuasion rather than threats, and in your love life things are occurring which are significant. During the next couple of days there may be brief encounters so you need to keep your eyes open wide, otherwise you could seriously miss out.

♏

29 TUESDAY There's a possibility that friends may let you down when you most need them, but you must not allow your temper to erupt like a volcano. Try to put yourself in their position, because in this way you'll be able to understand. Perhaps they have no intention of letting you down, but circumstances make it difficult for them to keep formal promises they had made to you.

30 WEDNESDAY Today finds you highly ambitious for one reason or another. The only trouble is that when focussing on ambition and worldly success you do tend to neglect most other areas of life. If you do so at the moment you can expect to hear some very loud complaints from those who mean a great deal to you. The answer is to try to create some kind of balance.

31 THURSDAY You seem to be in a happy-go-lucky mood today, passing on cheery news to other people and receiving a promise as well as plenty of compliments from the opposite sex. Naturally, some of you will be at work and, if so, things won't be as pleasant as they have been; there may be a clash between career interests and your leisure time. You've got a tough decision to make here but you must remember that you can't please all the people all the time, and if you attempt to do so, you're going to run yourself ragged.

NOVEMBER

The Sun will be making its way through the water sign of Scorpio up until 21 November and this, of course, is your time of the year and you can maximize your confidence with the near certainty that you are right over practically everything. But don't overdo this particular trend, will you?

♏

On 22 November, the Sun will be moving into Sagittarius, the area of your chart devoted to money. While this state of affairs exists, it looks as if you'll be keen to save your hard-earned cash rather than splashing out. We all, of course, need at least some time in the year when we can do this, otherwise we could find ourselves in the bankruptcy courts.

Mercury will also be sailing along in your sign until the 18th, making you far more flexible than is usual; this is no bad thing because you can lack this commodity from time to time. Because of Mercury you'll be able to appreciate other people's opinions and may even be handing on some wise advice. Hopefully, other people will listen, but if they don't there's nothing you can do about it except say to yourself, 'well I did warn them'. On the 19th Mercury moves on into the fiery sign of Sagittarius and this suggests that new financial opportunities may be in the offing. The trouble is, there is also the possibility of others chasing you for money owed.

Venus is in your sign all month, and really the stars are spoiling you. Not only do you have extra confidence but you're looking good, feeling good and at your most creative as well as amorous. If you should be single and meet anyone special during this period, the relationship could be long-lasting, so do stay alert.

Mars will be in Libra, a rather secretive part to your chart, so there is a possibility that underneath all of this confidence and self-belief you may not be quite as sure as you appear to be, but there's nothing wrong with questioning our behaviour from time to time, otherwise how can we possibly improve ourselves?

The pattern made by the stars seems to suggest that you'll be the 'initiator' of everything that occurs, so if things go wrong you'll only have yourself to blame, but just for once you'll take this on board and be a little more philosophical than is usually the case.

In many ways November is likely to be one of the best times of the year, so don't hang around feeling sorry for yourself, grab all opportunities that come your way in any area and you'll be making the most out of your stars.

1 FRIDAY What you thought was merely a passive resistance to your plans is turning out to be far more serious. Other people are not going to let you get away with anything less than a compromise. Again and again you seem to have to please everyone, rather than yourself. For once, stand by your own ideals. After all, they are no less valuable than anybody else's; all you've got to do is believe this.

2 SATURDAY Envious twittering from certain people is only proving how right you are to follow a chosen path. Your motivation regarding your business affairs is also admirable. If you don't pull out all the stops, others will have more than enough ammunition to lob back at you. You're on to a good thing, so make sure it's you who has the last laugh.

3 SUNDAY Although you're feeling persuasive, it would be much better to keep your mind-blowing thoughts to yourself. You'll find the stars today are forcing you to get everything out of proportion. The last thing you want is to start putting people off just when you're about to embark on a major coup.

4 MONDAY Today is the day of the new Moon and it occurs in your sign so you're probably feeling pretty good about yourself. This is an ideal time for making new beginnings for everyone, but they are most important for you with the new

Moon in your sign. Take your courage in both hands and push ahead; you really can't go wrong, not even if you try.

5 TUESDAY Someone is asking you to do them a favour today. Of course, you usually agree after serious contemplation, but this time it's in your interests to discover their motives. Any dealing with irresponsible or naive people should be finalized quickly. You don't want to be their life support system for too long.

6 WEDNESDAY Assistance from other people is fine when you know that they are simply trying to put your mind at ease, but not so welcome when they're actually trying to manipulate you. On the surface, what you're being offered seems quite genuinely thoughtful. Take care, however, you're not gullible, but you would be wise to think carefully about their reasoning before accepting.

7 THURSDAY Focus on a project that gets you in touch with someone you want to impress. You're about to experience a fascinating creative turn of events, and such an important contact promises wider exposure. Stay firm and decisive – you don't want others to lead you astray. You know your ideas are winners, so play them for all you can.

8 FRIDAY If others are being awkward or playing hard to get, don't assume it's your fault. You are not responsible for every move regarding one close relationship. All this getting nowhere fast at least gives you time to contemplate their behaviour.

♏

9 SATURDAY Anyone doubting your word concerning a close relationship doesn't understand you. But with your amazing capacity for forward thinking, you can be positive and inspiring. It won't be long before people realize that when you put your mind to it, you can come up with answers – especially where your happiness is involved. Put your case forward.

10 SUNDAY Don't give up on something in your working life because everyone thinks you should. You have enough confidence to pull the idea off, however cagey you are about doing so. It's likely you will discover that there's abundant joy in being true to your principles, rather than following the herd. Of course, hearsay is fascinating, but self-belief is beautiful.

11 MONDAY Foolproof though a certain joint transaction seems, it could become a bone of contention. The planets are urging you to take a serious approach, rather than maintaining a passive attitude. Results will be forthcoming but only if you realize that others want to take control of the situation. Show you actually mean business – for your own sake.

12 TUESDAY The planets' influences are compelling you to express feelings to someone special. It's not that you want to make a drama out of it, but the emotional tension you're under just needs to be diffused. Of course, you have the courage to say what's on your mind. But rather than make a big thing of it, be magical and seductive; it's more liberating.

13 WEDNESDAY Financial problems aside, you're being tested in your ability to handle certain funds. Recognizing limitations of the material aspects of your life is proving a problem. But you're not hampered by anyone other than yourself. Yes, of course, it's hard to keep track of it all, but with a new insight you can improve the situation.

14 THURSDAY Stay in touch with those who have your interests at heart. You've been in danger of cutting a few ties, simply because there are so many other important changes going on in your life. And, of course, you must attend to those, too. If others realize you're as sincere in your trust in them as you are with yourself, then you'll be rewarded with more than your share of happiness. And there will be plenty of opportunities in store that will surprise you.

15 FRIDAY Today the stars are certainly throwing your judgement completely out the window. Best then to shelve important matters for the time being and turn your attention to putting the finishing touches to jobs, both at home and at work. Successes hold strong appeal this evening, and whether you give in to this or not much depends on the size of your bank account. You should also bear in mind the effect this is likely to have on your health.

16 SATURDAY This is the time for going after what you want, whether it's ambition, romance or money. You should have extra confidence and solar power, which draws other people to you. So this is not a time for putting other's interests before your own; this is one period in the year when you must insist on being a little selfish; hard for you, but imperative if you are to make the most of your time.

17 SUNDAY You're going to find it much easier to realize your secret hopes and wishes, although you may need to do so with an eye for the practical side of life. There's nothing you can't achieve; all you have to do is have a little faith. If you're fancy free, no doubt it has been difficult for you to find a suitable mate. Don't worry, because soon you'll be meeting someone with whom you can share your deepest emotions as well as your interests.

18 MONDAY It might be a good idea to pick the brains of other people, because they are at their most imaginative and intuitive and are willing to lend a helping hand, should it be needed. If you're in a steady relationship, you can expect to get loads of attention from the special person in your life. This evening, you go to sleep with a smile on your face, so that can't be too bad.

19 TUESDAY Imagination is strong today, so any creative or romantic activity should go well. What's more, it's a perfect time for discarding old habits, out-dated ideas and any clutter that's littering your home or your life. This evening, forget about those work problems and concentrate on having fun. It's true that others have been trying to undermine your ego and highlight hidden obstacles which lie ahead, but nothing is going to stop you from enjoying yourself 100 percent.

20 WEDNESDAY Today is the day of the full Moon and it occurs in the earthy sign of Taurus. That, of course, is your opposite number, so you may find that other people are being downright awkward and perverse. Best to leave them alone, they've problems of their own, and get on with what has to be done. They'll soon come around to your way of thinking, all you've got to do is hang on.

Monthly and Daily Guides: November

21 THURSDAY You must be prepared for literally anything. There could be phone calls from people you haven't heard from in simply ages but, nevertheless, you are delighted to speak to them. Others may drop around on a whim and again they'll find a warm welcome waiting for them. This evening is an ideal time for sporting activities and also party-going, but don't go out looking for the love of your life, Scorpio – if the person is there, he or she will soon find you.

22 FRIDAY Today the Sun will be moving into the fiery sign of Sagittarius and that is the area of your chart devoted to cash, so for the remainder of the month you are going to be into 'saving and conserving' rather than spending in a crazy way.

23 SATURDAY Today you appear to be hunting around for bargains and they will be difficult to find. Money spent on entertainment this evening will be good value and, although romance has a flirty feel about it, I wouldn't go out looking for Romeo or Juliet, not just yet anyway.

24 SUNDAY The stars are certainly livening up your grey matter. The only problem is, you could become more than usually impulsive over the next couple of weeks, which could mean that mistakes will be made, particularly where paperwork is concerned. Slow down when involving yourself with anything of an intricate nature and in that way you'll be able to avoid a great deal of time wasting.

25 MONDAY Clearly today is a time to shelve all thinking and planning and leap into action. Wherever you go, you will find a warm welcome, not only for yourself but also for your ideas. Those of you chasing work will be making a big impression and should be lucky. For other Scorpios love life looks promising too.

26 TUESDAY You can expect the maximum cooperation from other people at work and at home, so this is a time to call in a few favours if necessary, or maybe pick somebody else's brain who can, perhaps, add something special to a project or idea of yours. This evening, whatever you do, make certain that you don't confuse a sexual attraction for romance – an easy mistake for any Scorpio. Satisfy your appetites by all means, but be careful and, above all else, don't deceive yourself.

27 WEDNESDAY You may be thinking you are in for a quiet day, but nothing could be further from the truth. The telephone leaps into action, the doorbell never stops ringing and other people pop in quite unexpectedly. Mind you, you won't mind too much because at least this will give you an excuse to leave household chores to one side for the time being. The chance to go to a party this evening could lead to romance, so for heaven's sake accept.

28 THURSDAY It's best to avoid the company of friends and acquaintances because if you don't, I'm afraid they'll only bring you down. They seem to be in a state of depression for one reason or another and, although you are one of the most helpful signs of the zodiac, you also are one person who is easily put upon from time to time. There are occasions when you need to put your foot down and this could very well be one of them, otherwise you'll end this day at a very low ebb.

29 FRIDAY Other people are bursting with good ideas, originality and charisma. Well, you're one sign that can work successfully in harness and this is exactly the way you should be travelling at this particular time. This evening make sure you keep a high profile, because a strong attraction is likely to flare up and take you by surprise.

30 SATURDAY If you've been trying to catch the eye of a member of the opposite sex, you'll succeed. New people you meet will play a big role in your life for some time to come so greet with them with a friendly smile. Avoid the glitzy shops today because you're in danger of spending more than you can realistically afford. It seems, too, that you are itching to make a fresh start in some way as well as busily thinking of new ways of earning cash. All in all a hectic time.

DECEMBER

The Sun will be drifting along in the fiery sign of Sagittarius up until 21 December, and that's the area of your chart devoted to money and your earning power. You seem to be doing very well for yourself in the materialistic side to life, thank you very much.

On 22 December the Sun will be moving into Capricorn and that's the area of your life devoted to the mind, which is going to be extremely keen and very shrewd, so you'll be doing some good bargaining. Furthermore, it is also a good time for special shopping and for popping in and out of the homes of friends and contacts which will generate a lot of goodwill.

From 9 December onwards, Mercury will be in Capricorn, so it's going to be very difficult for you to sit still. There will be lots of little reasons for seeing other people and casual romance seems to be the norm rather than the exception. If you've a brother or sister with whom you have fallen out recently, now is the time for kissing and making up, so see what you can do.

Venus is situated in Scorpio all month – you lucky thing – so that means you're going to be looking good, feeling good and full of confidence. If you're artistic you'll be putting forward some good work and, of course, romance is exceptionally well starred, maybe even to the point of engagement or marriage.

Mars is also in your sign from the 2nd, and this will be geeing up your sexuality to the point where you can think of little else. If you have a partner, they're certainly going to be kept busy; if not, you're going to be very popular with the opposite sex. Furthermore, Mars in your sign could make you a little bit bad tempered and tense, so if you flare up and insult someone I'm afraid you're going to have to apologize at a later date – but then that's par for the course, isn't it?

The pattern made by the stars seems to suggest that you'll be starting many relationships, projects and ideas, but may lack follow through. This is no way to travel, Scorpio, as you know deep down. If you're going to become inefficient you can't expect to get the proverbial pat on the back, which you're used to, so double check everything because with your pride it wouldn't do for somebody else to point out your mistakes – not easy for you to swallow, is it?

1 SUNDAY No matter how enthusiastic and helpful other people seem they are unlikely to be able to tell you exactly where they stand at the moment, or even whether you can count on them. In no way, however, should this cause you to

Monthly and Daily Guides: December

question their intentions, integrity or sincerity. Matters completely beyond their control are the only thing that is holding them back and as soon as the path ahead is clear they'll be on your side, never fear.

2 MONDAY This is the day when you may develop an unusual need for freedom and independence which will no doubt surprise other people who thought they knew you well. You're more physically active than is usually the case and, on the romantic front, there'll be more than just a few brief encounters over the next few days, but you shouldn't take any of them too seriously.

3 TUESDAY You're in an emotional mood today, which will be appreciated by those who love you, but you must try to cast away the past and look towards the future. Luckily, you're feeling more optimistic than you have been for some time, but because of your current mood you'll want more 'people contact'. You may find it difficult to reach others on the phone, so why not take a chance on an impromptu visit. Romance could also be taking off this evening with someone you've known for a long time.

4 WEDNESDAY To a degree you can deal with fiddling details without getting irritated or hot under the collar. This evening it's likely you'll want to talk over differences with a loved one, who'll be surprised at your confrontational mood – why not act out of character, Scorpio, because it'll stop people taking you for granted for a change? If you're entertaining at home this evening you've certainly picked a good time.

♏

5 THURSDAY The stars could put you in a pessimistic mood, but always remember, Scorpio, if you expect the worst you may wish it down upon you, so try to think thoughts of sunshine instead. Wherever possible spend time with people who can lift your spirits and make you laugh; a good giggle does wonders for your mood and even helps you to release tension, which can't be bad.

6 FRIDAY Circumstances are encouraging you to face up to an emotional partnership problem head on and to make others understand they are living in a fantasy world. Events that took place a while ago made your position clear, and you probably believed companions would eventually come to their senses. They haven't, and you must now think of your own comfort, happiness and security.

7 SATURDAY You may be strongly tempted to take on more responsibilities right now, especially if cash gains are in the offing. Do try to be satisfied with your achievements and resist the temptation to keep on pushing for more. Be sure that you get out this evening as the stars are insisting that you relax and have fun, mainly because romance is in the air.

8 SUNDAY Those closest to you could be insecure, moody and generally uncooperative. The best thing you can do is to detach yourself and go about your own business because their mood will soon change. If you're in the throes of any DIY, don't leave tools or implements hanging around otherwise there could be accidents.

9 MONDAY Today Mercury will be moving into the earthy sign of Capricorn and that's the area of your chart devoted to short trips and the affairs of brothers and sisters. Any chance to travel for the sake of work should be grabbed with both hands because it will benefit you in the long run. Furthermore, if you have a Gemini or a Virgo in your life they're going to be occupying centre stage and you must control any envious urges that you experience.

10 TUESDAY At work there may be rumours that important changes are taking place and you might feel put out because you haven't been consulted. What's more, you need to curb your urge to elaborate on other people's mistakes. If you do, there's no reason why you shouldn't be in clover. On a more personal level, you're more emotional than is usually the case, so when it comes to tackling family problems you may have to put your feelings to one side.

11 WEDNESDAY You mustn't allow yourself to become so bogged down by your own feelings that you believe others don't understand, because this would be wrong; the stars suggest that those closest to you are only too willing to listen to what you have to say. Providing you can overcome this mood, it could be a great time for making changes and also for coming clean and admitting that, perhaps, you've gone off in the wrong direction.

12 THURSDAY This is a time for resting, reflecting and rejuvenating, despite the fact that this might go against your sociable nature; plus, of course, you hate to feel you might be missing out on something good. Still, if you can sort out your jumbled thoughts, just remember that this is a time when whatever Scorpio wants, Scorpio can have.

13 FRIDAY Today it's important to build on an opportunity that comes your way. If you let it slide you may not get another chance. On the other hand, in your personal life, you may be confronted with a new kind of problem and will be feeling your way. This difficulty may arise because lately you have been far too preoccupied with pulling yourself up the ladder of success. If this is the case, the stars suggest you turn your attention to a special someone in your life.

14 SATURDAY You'll instinctively know what needs to be done on the working front and usually won't be in a lather of confusion where emotions are concerned. You'll find it a good deal easier to let other people know how you feel about them. You would usually wait in the background hoping they'll notice you, but not now; there could be a few surprised faces.

15 SUNDAY You may be hearing from an official source which might fill you with horror, but don't jump the gun or anticipate the worst; continue to think positively and you'll discover that you'll be able to influence the tide of events in your favour. It's a great time for a spot of bargain hunting, and an even better time for those at home, especially if you want to get in touch with brothers and sisters.

16 MONDAY The stars put you in a very energetic frame of mind. If you work manually or are involved with sports, you can expect a certain amount of success. There's a coming together between yourself and others and this is perhaps one of the best days of the week for romance. And if you've decided to become engaged or married very soon, you've been very clever indeed. If not, make sure you keep a high profile because that special person may be lurking around in the corner.

♏

17 TUESDAY Today is the time when you really must promise yourself that you will be more independent, stand on your own two feet and knock on doors until the right one is opened. Any challenging aspects during the day ahead can't thwart, harm or tame you, as long as you keep your eye on the ball.

18 WEDNESDAY You're seriously beginning to wonder whether or not you want to continue a current relationship. It might be a good idea to avoid making that decision today, wait a little longer and if feelings have not changed it could be that you're wasting your time. Unless you can be sure of somebody else's devotion and commitment, you could be setting yourself up for a hurtful time.

19 THURSDAY Taking on change is difficult but you shouldn't have too much of a problem today because the stars are in a cooperative mood. As usual, making decisions proves to be a bit of a problem because one minute you feel lost and the next minute excited by the way things are developing. Yet no matter how strange or peculiar things may seem, you must believe that there is a method to the stars' madness and at a later stage everything will fall into place.

20 FRIDAY Change is not one of your favourite words because it invariably leads to a certain amount of inner conflict: you're so worried about doing the wrong thing that sometimes you don't act at all. But, like it or not, this is no time for brushing aside the opportunity to follow a new direction, to shake off what is old and familiar and to confront the world with a certain degree of vulnerability, as well as a bright optimism.

♏

21 SATURDAY Where to go, who to spend your time with and what to do – you may be driving yourself completely up the wall and down the other side. The thing to do is to start off your day quietly, sit down and work out what you'd like to do and who you would like for company. Ideally, it needs to be someone who can make you laugh, otherwise the whole day could go to waste and that would be a pity.

22 SUNDAY Today the Sun will be moving into Capricorn and that's the area of your chart devoted to the affairs of brothers and sisters, short journeys and casual romance. For the rest of the year you seem to be enjoying yourself and are not quite as intense as you usually are, much to the relief of other people. Enjoy a new-found popularity.

23 MONDAY Your sense of justice may be offended today because it will seem to you that somebody keeps moving the goalposts and you must decide whether you want to continue playing their game at all. However, right now, the stars suggest that you don't have to fit in with other people's rules, regulations or plans. What happens may surprise you, but really there is no cause for panic; you are the one with all the answers, so get out the thinking cap.

24 TUESDAY This, of course, is Christmas Eve and no doubt you are rushing around trying to get everybody organized. However, what you don't realize is that other people do have minds of their own and they're quite capable of sorting themselves out, so you just worry about your own affairs and let others get on with theirs.

Monthly and Daily Guides: December

25 WEDNESDAY HAPPY CHRISTMAS. On this important day the Moon is in the sign of Virgo and that's the area of your chart devoted to friends and contacts. That is extremely apt, because although you may be having one or two relatives around for a short time, there is likely to be a constant stream of friends and acquaintances will be dropping in, which you will thoroughly enjoy.

26 THURSDAY Today's stars seem to suggest that you may run into a little trouble, possibly due to the fact that others are doing their best to push you around and test your loyalty. You really can't put up with any kind of under-handed behaviour or emotional blackmail and you'll be very quick to let other people know this. Don't worry too much about this; the stars will certainly help you to stand by your principles, so don't be afraid to do just that.

27 FRIDAY It's time for asking yourself some questions and one of them should be whether you should just go along with friends or workmates, whose actions seem to be a little on the desperate side. The stars are suggesting that as a Scorpio you're being far too pedantic. Don't allow yourself to take things too far otherwise you'll be losing out on the popularity stakes and that would be a great pity.

28 SATURDAY Even if your efforts to get others to be straight with you about their feelings and intentions have been unrewarding, try once again. As long as you can persuade yourself to do so, revelations you receive could be surprising to everyone and they'll certainly be giving you something to talk about.

♏

29 SUNDAY On a social level it's important that you accept all invitations this evening because you are likely to meet some new: interesting people who could help you to secure one of your longed-for ambitions. This is likely to apply professionally, as well as personally. It may be officially a holiday period but that won't stop your contacts getting in touch with you.

30 MONDAY You seem to be in something of a dither, running around trying to make arrangements, perhaps for tomorrow. Other people seem to be unsure as to whether they're going to meet up with you and you might be tempted to 'blow your stack'. That is not the way to go, Scorpio. The best thing to do is to calm down, turn on the charm and then they really won't be able to resist you and you'll be able to sort everything out without rancour.

31 TUESDAY This is, of course, New Year's Eve, and there's nobody better than a Scorpio at going to extremes, whether it's with booze, sex or fun and games. Mind you, if you have a mate, of course, such behaviour is not desirable, but if you haven't, well then why not please yourself and throw caution to the wind? Lastly, the usual caution not to drink and drive, especially as, if you do so on this particular New Year's Eve, you will be in trouble.

HAPPY NEW YEAR.

Your Birth Chart by Teri King

A Book of Life

Simply fill in your details on the form below for an interpretation of your birth chart compiled by TERI KING. Your birth chart will be supplied bound and personalized. Each chart costs £30.00 sterling – add £1.50 sterling for postage if you live outside the UK. Please make your cheque or postal order (cash is not accepted) payable to *Kingstar* and send together with your form to the following address: 6 Elm Grove Road, Barnes, London SW13 0BT, England.

Date of Birth _____ Time of Birth _____

Place of Birth _____

Country of Birth _____

Name _____

Address _____

_____

_____ Postcode _____

A birth chart also makes an ideal present! Why not include, on a separate sheet, the details of a friend or member of your family? Include £30.00 for each extra chart.

Thorsons
Directions for life

www.thorsons.com

The latest mind, body and spirit news

Exclusive author interviews

Read extracts from the latest books

Join in mind-expanding discussions

Win great prizes every week

Thorsons catalogue & ordering service

www.thorsons.com